How to draw

NeoPopRealism

INK images

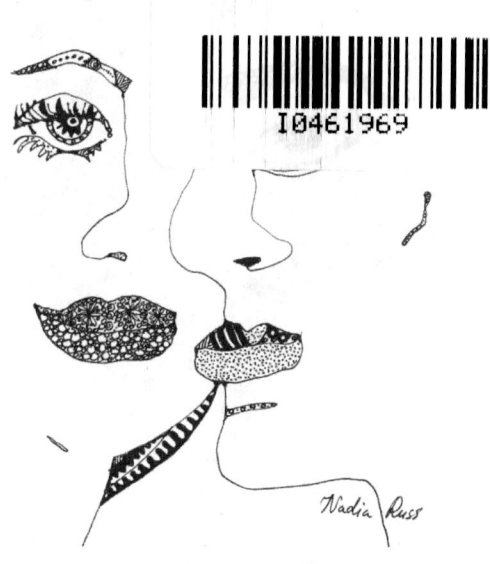

Basics

NADIA RUSS

NeoPopRealism PRESS

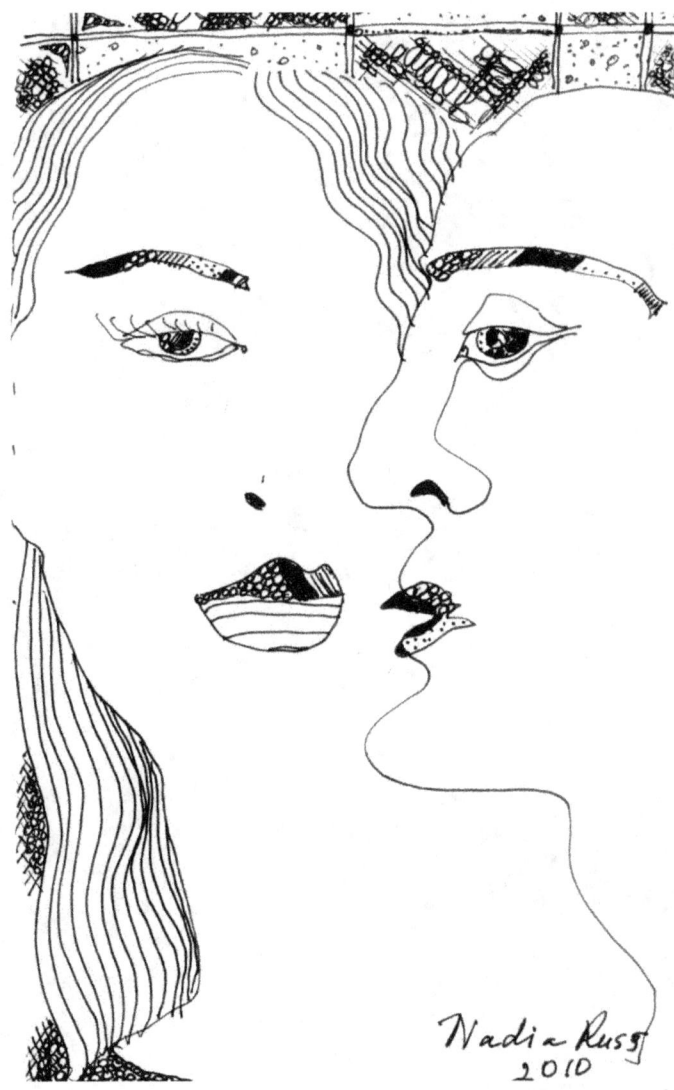

Nadia Russ, *Faces*, Ink on paper, 5.5"x 8", 2010

A book *"How to Draw NeoPopRealism Ink Images: Basics"* by NeoPopRealism PRESS with illustrations by Nadia Russ takes reader/artist on an enlightening and life-changing journey to finding passion and happiness in one's life.

How to draw

NeoPopRealism

INK images

Basics

NADIA RUSS
NeoPopRealism **PRESS**

First published in 2011 by NeoPopRealism PRESS
PO BOX 366
New York, NY 10013

NeopoprealismPress@mail.com

"*How to Draw NeoPopRealism Ink Images: Basics*" by Nadia RUSS (aka Nadejda Maloletneva)
Illustrations by Nadia Russ

Published in the United States of America
Language: English

ISBN-13: 978-0615515755
ISBN-10: 0615515754

11 12 13 14 15   10 9 8 7 6 5 4 3 2 1

This book teaches how to draw NeoPopRealism ink images.
For teenagers and adults.

www.neopoprealism.org

CONTENT

INTRODUCTION

NeoPopRealism ink drawing concept was created by Nadia Russ in 1989.

It was an experiment. She was trying to connect to the Universe and let the Universe use her as a Conductor when she created her drawings. She didn't want to follow any other artists' achievements, she decided to create absolutely new art form, like Picasso (Cubism), Dali (Surrealism), Andy Warhol (Pop Art) and a few other worldwide known artists had done.

Nadia Russ took her ink pen and began to draw a flowing line that turned into shapes, figures, often faces. Then, some sections (or all), that appeared, she filled with the repetitive patterns. She never uses eraser because if a mistake made, it disappears with the following repetitive patterns that balance the whole composition. Her work was unique, no one did anything like this before.

Later, January 4, 2003, Nadia Russ created a word NeoPopRealism and internationally announced new style of visual arts.

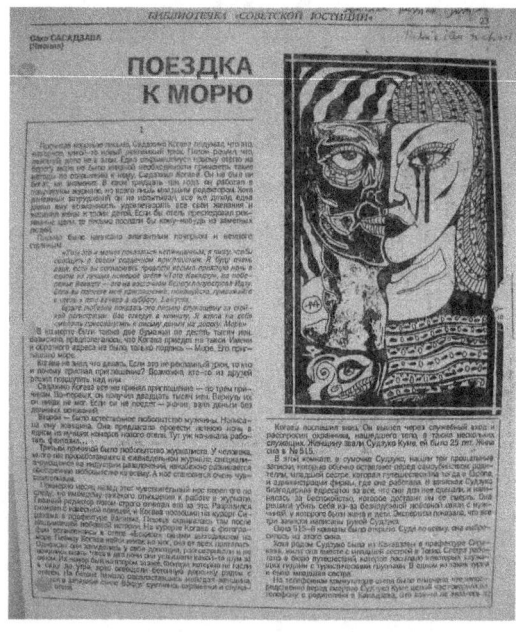

Nadia Russ illustrated a story by Saho Sasadzava for the *Russian Justice* Journal, 1992, Moscow, Russia

Get inspired

Whitney you focus on success, you fall into the trap of comparing yourself to others, feeling envious. Instead, focus on getting better every day, focus on excellence. Gratitude floods your body and brain with emotions that uplift you and energize you. Use your strengths for a bigger purpose beyond yourself. Focus on what you are giving instead of what you are getting, it makes every your step more rewarding and meaningful.

Get black ink pen *Foray Rolle Rollerball Medium 0.7 mm* or *Sharpie* and piece of cardstock paper 8.5"x11". Cut paper into two pieces - 5.5"x8.5" each. Now, you need one piece.

You would like to create something very unique and that's not always easy to do. You need to learn how to connect to the Universe and open your mind to the higher powers.

Close your eyes for a moment. Imaging that your consciousness leaves your body and fly to the Space where there are no people there but only super speed and super powers. Forget about your daily life experiences with supermarkets and laundry stations. No noise should disturb you except, possible, music. You are not you any more, you are a part of the Universe.

Slowly open your eyes. Try not to look around, look only at your piece of plain white paper. This is the beginning. . . Now draw.

If you after all couldn't draw NeoPopRealism image, go to the next pages of this book. After you learn how to draw with the all offered tips and tricks, come back to this page again and let see what will happen.

How to create a simplified ink drawing

The following pages will show you how to create step-by-step a simplified NeoPopRealism ink drawing "*The Flower*". You need no special skills. If you can draw line, circles, triangle, square, oval, you will be able to create this drawing. Every following image includes new details. The complete image looks like this:

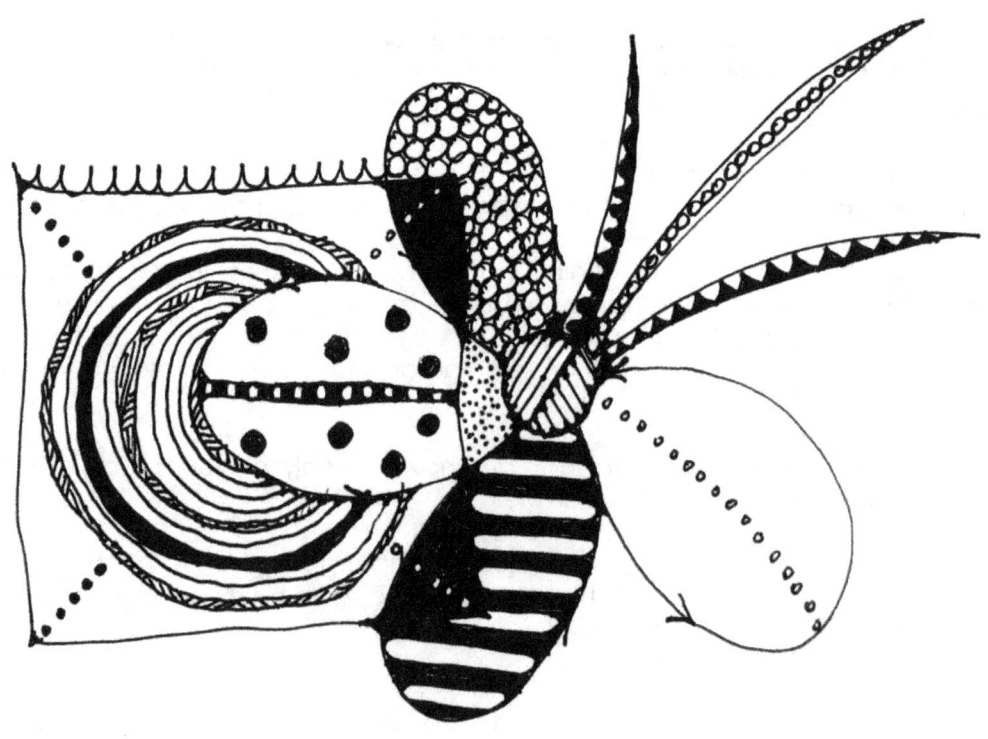

"*The Flower*", ink on paper, 8.5"x5.5"

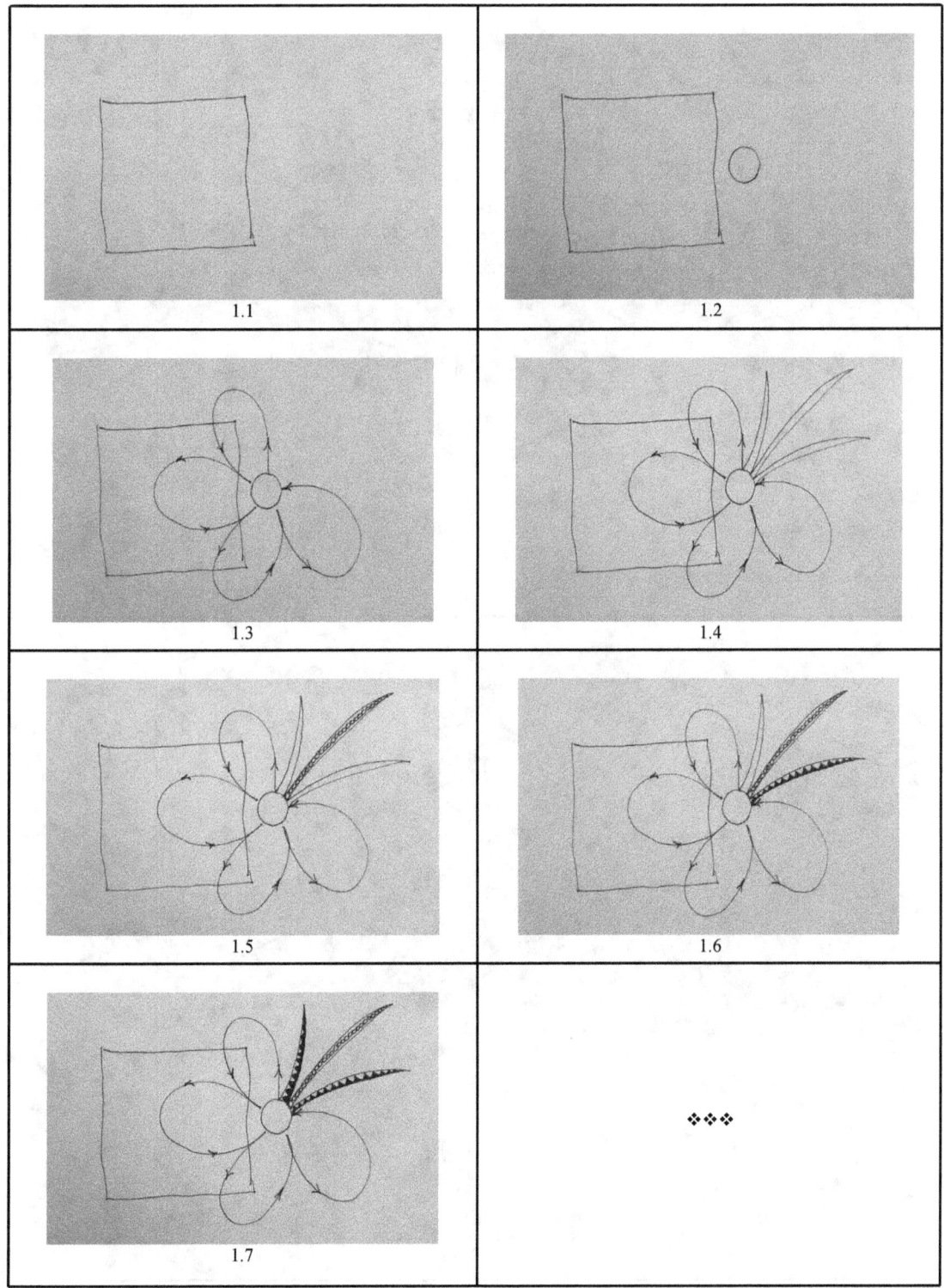

1.1

1.2

1.3

1.4

1.5

1.6

1.7

❖ ❖ ❖

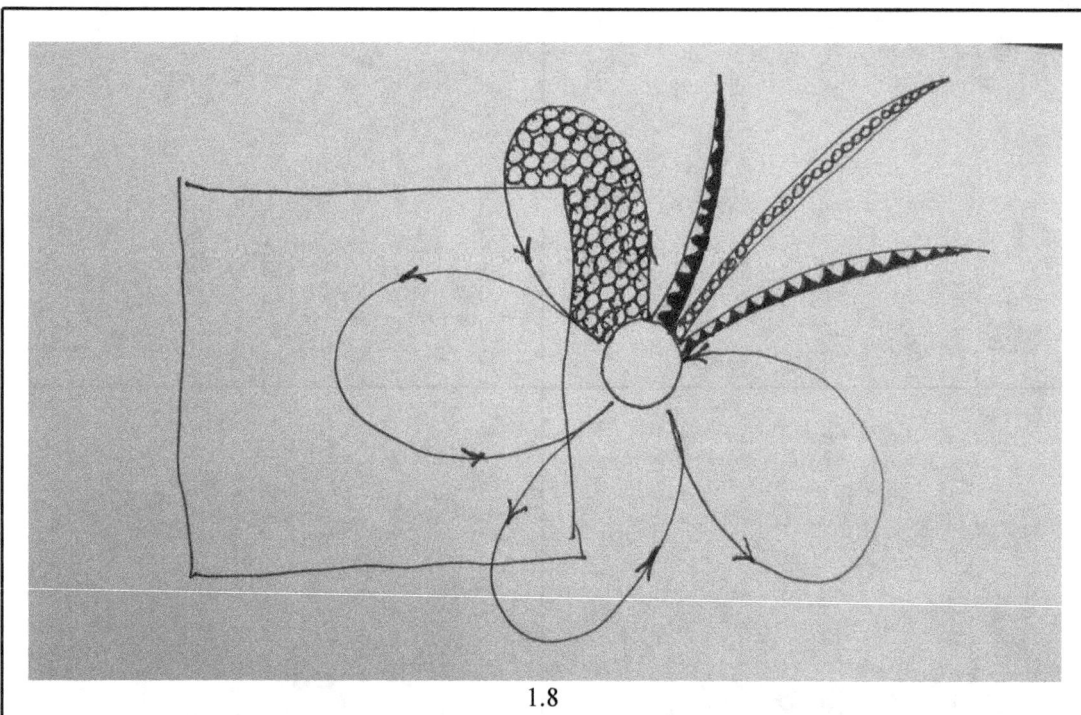

1.8

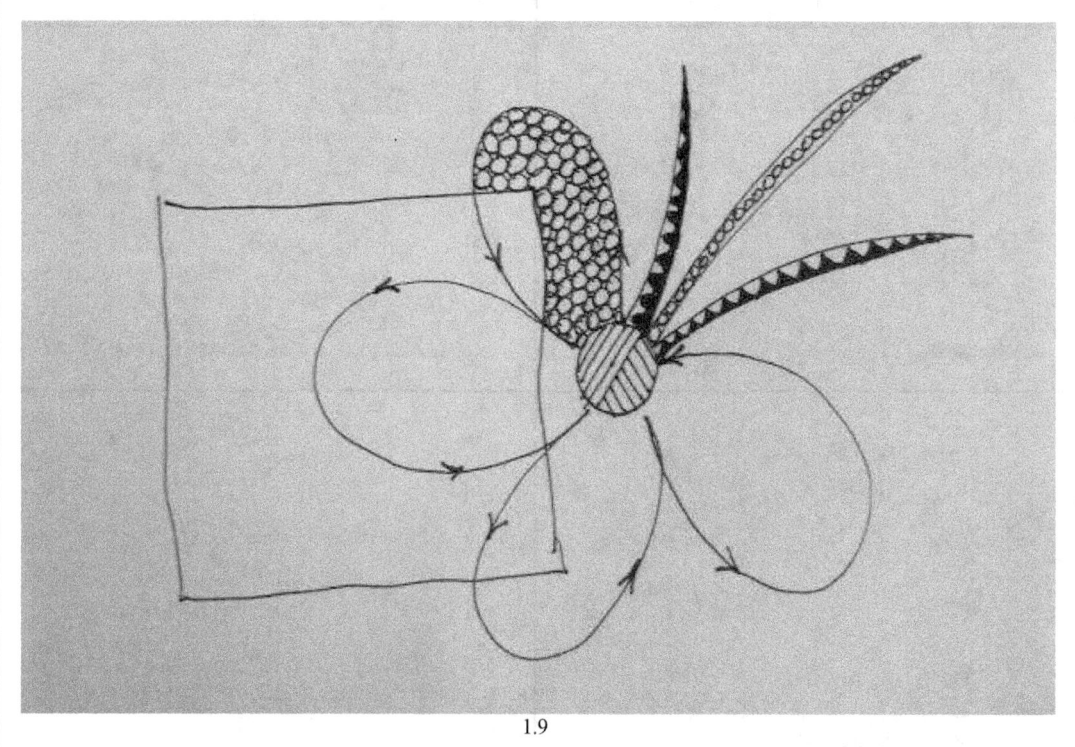

1.9

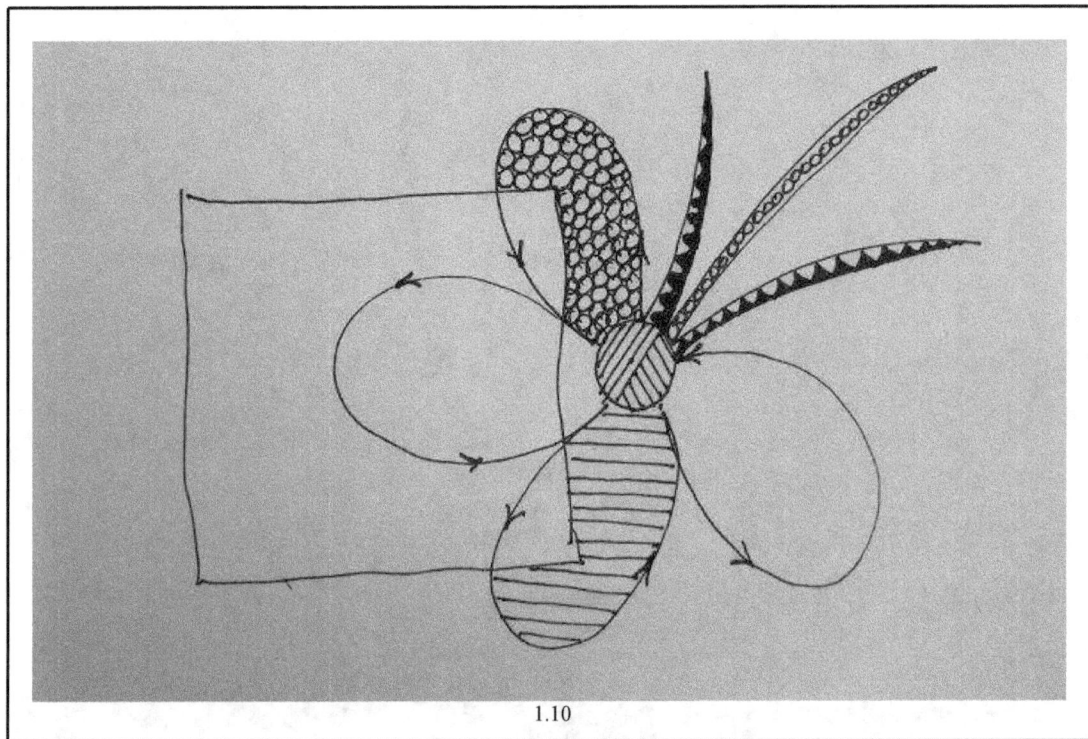

1.10

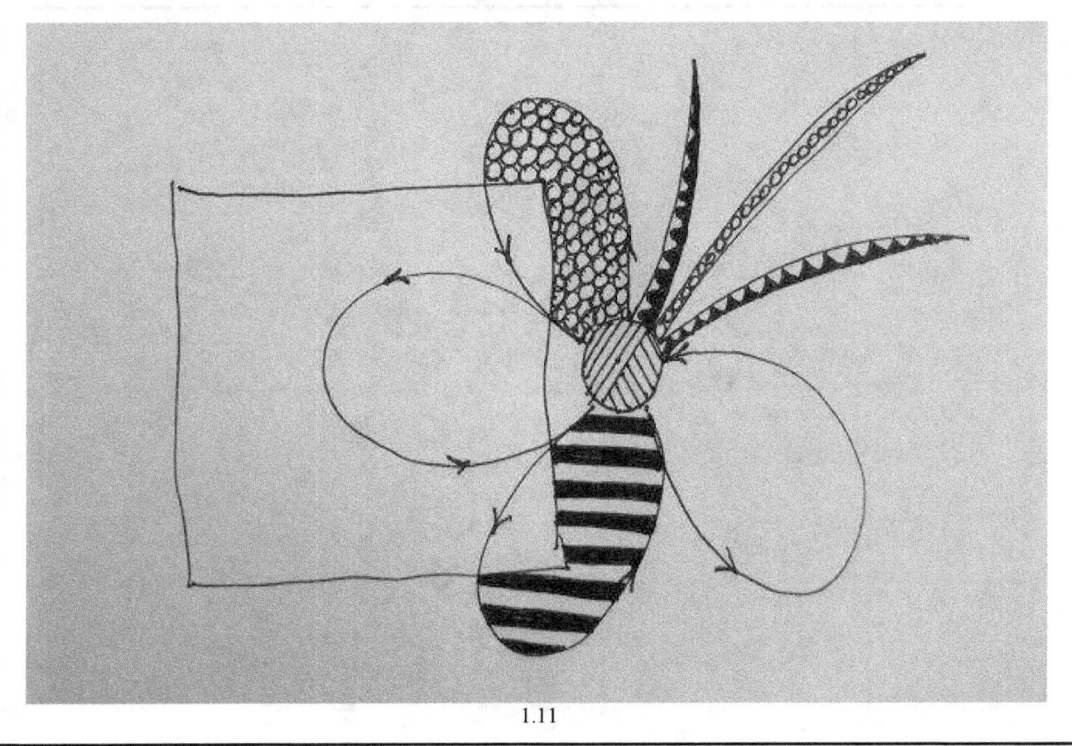

1.11

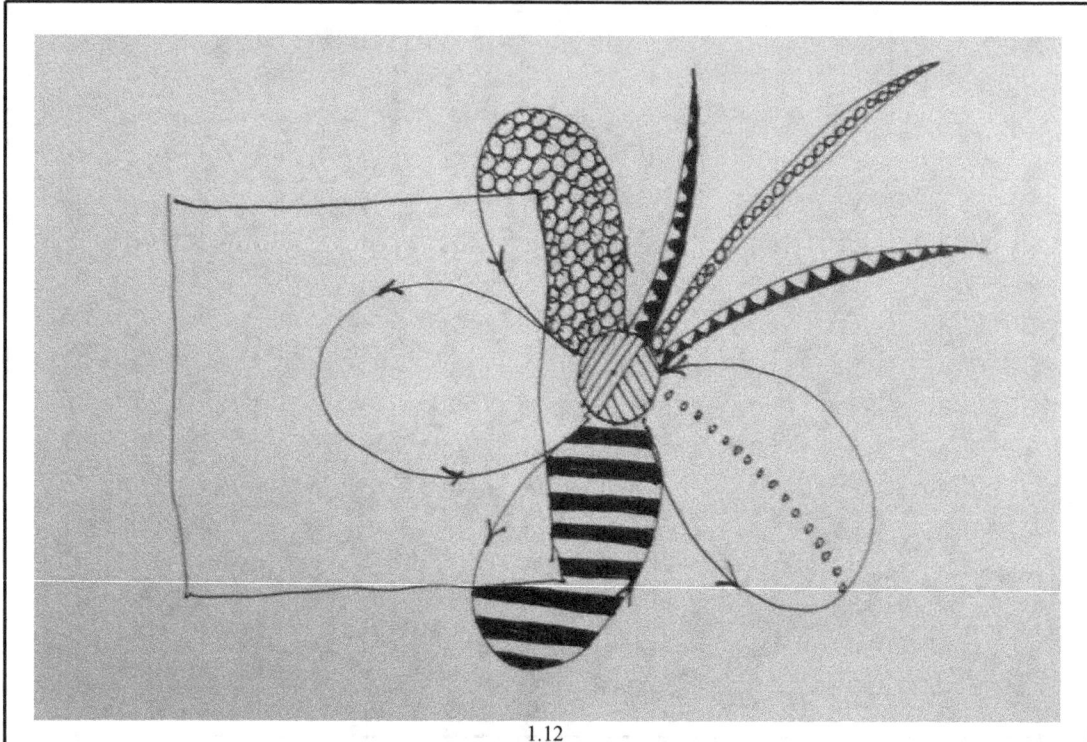

1.12

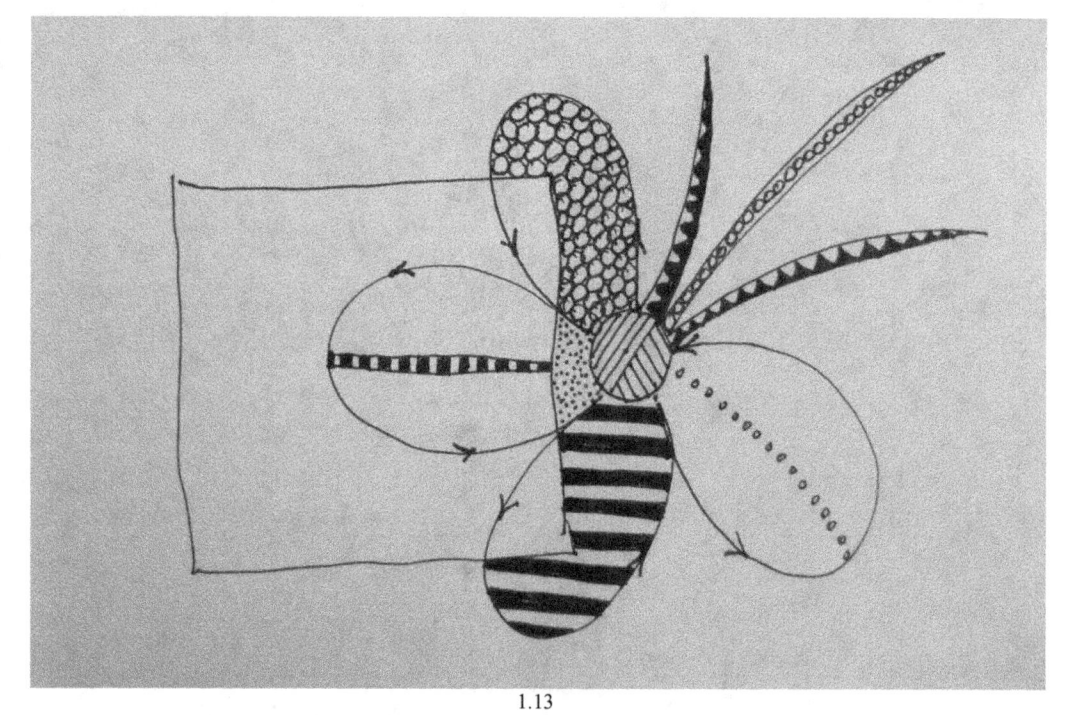

1.13

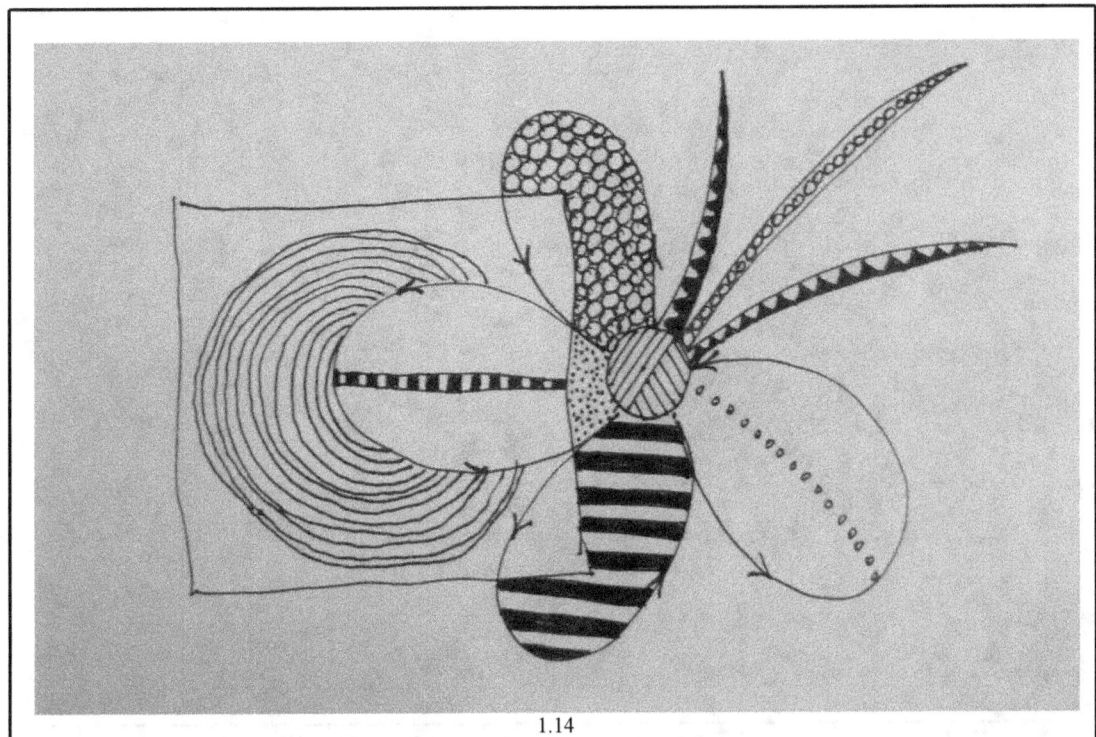

1.14

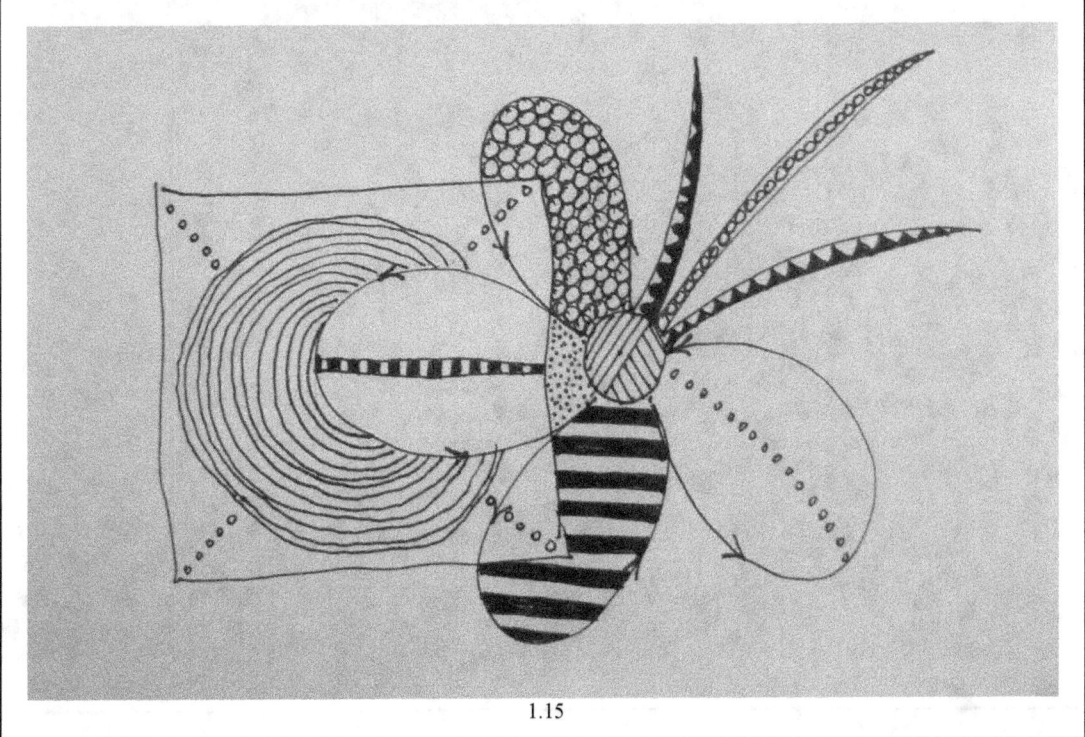

1.15

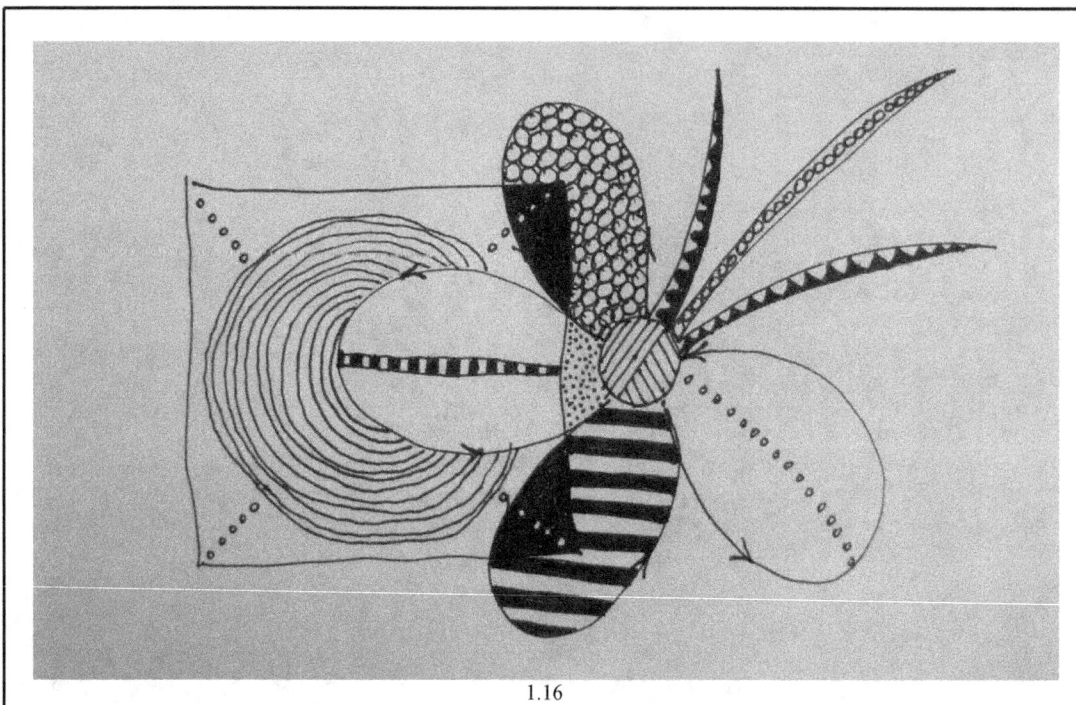

1.16

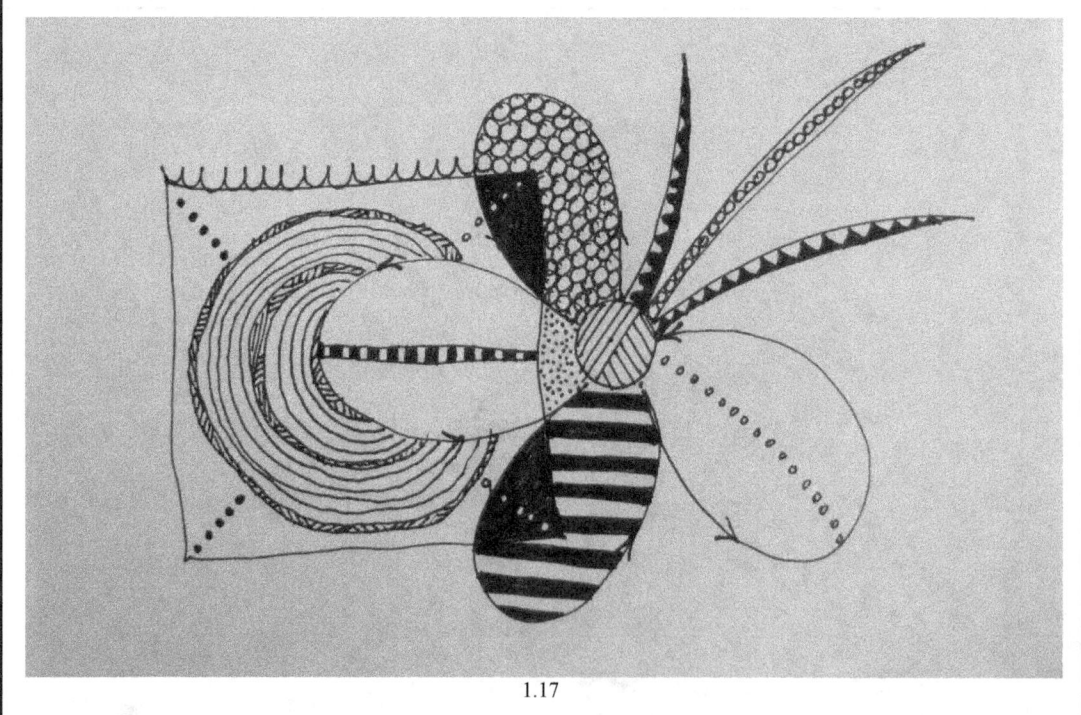

1.17

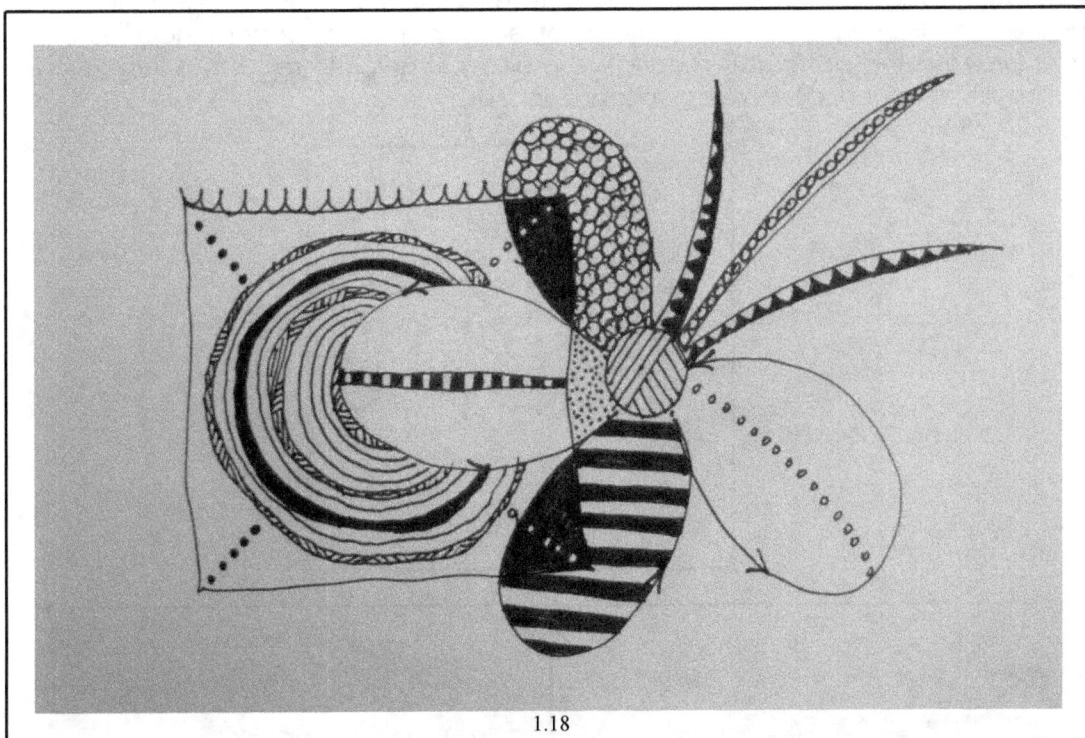

1.18

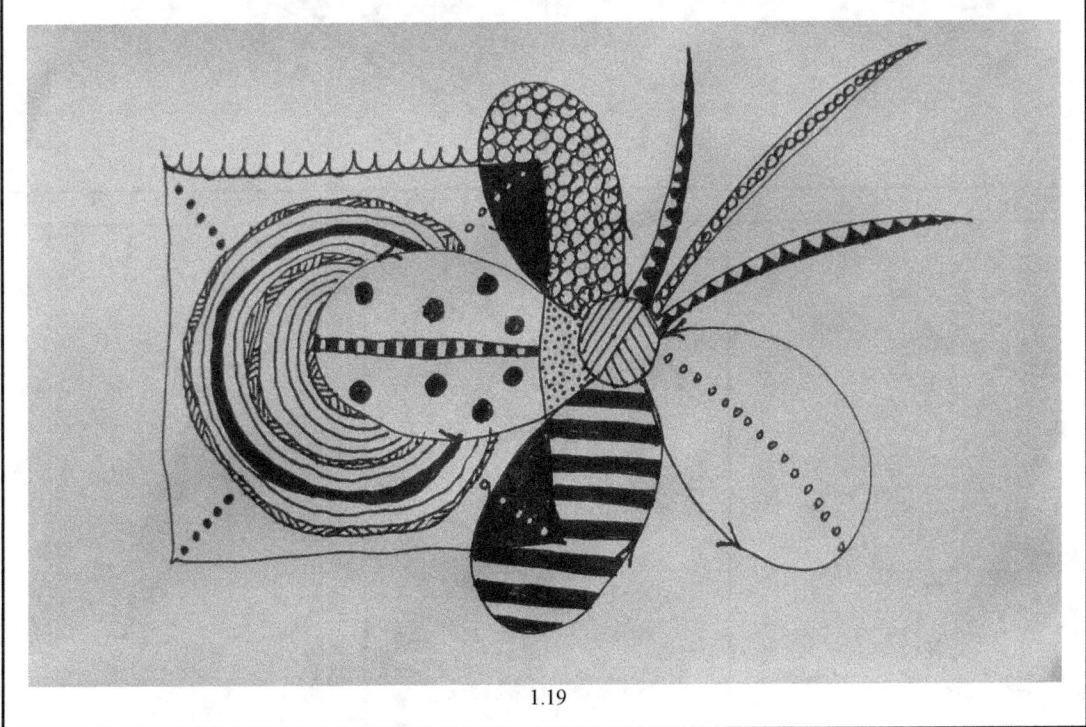

1.19

The following pages will show how to draw repetitive patterns, used in NeoPopRealism ink drawing "*The Flower.*" Every next image of each particular pattern includes one new detail. Drawing the patterns is meditative process, it helps to relax and increase brain's functionality as much, as develop your artistic skills.

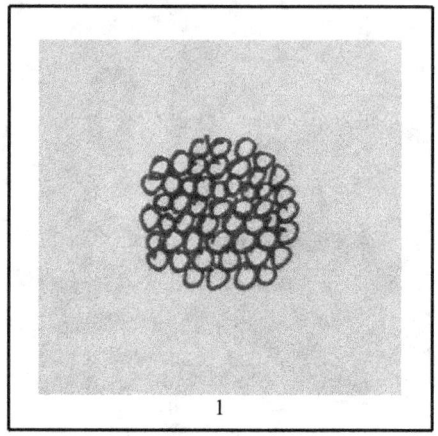

1

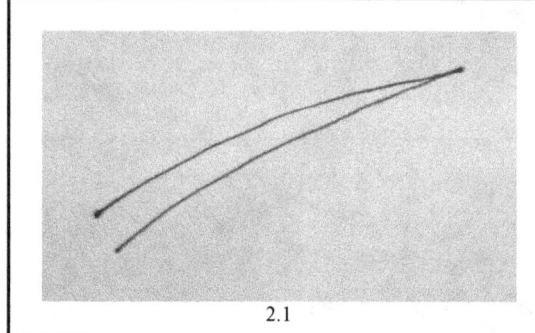

2.1

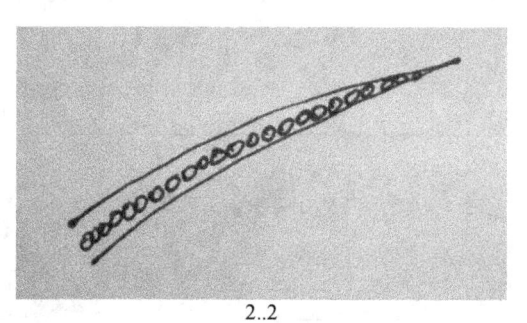

2..2

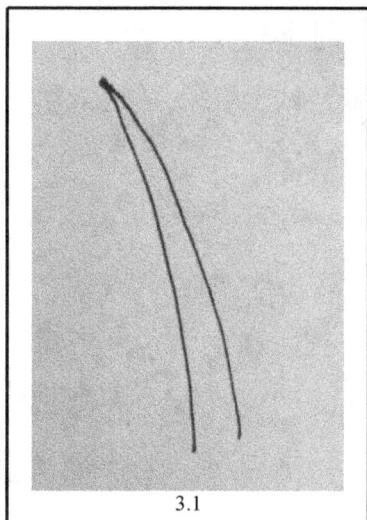

3.1

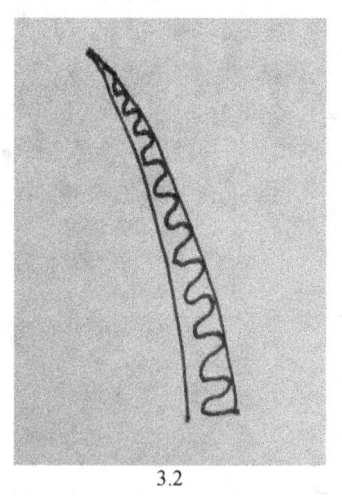

3.2

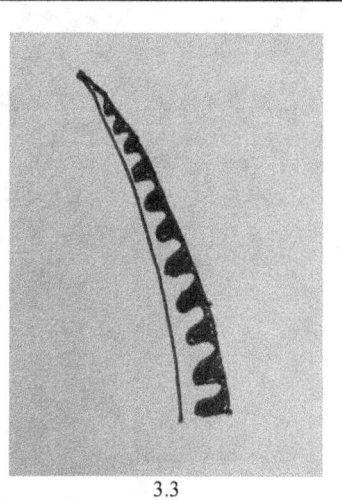

3.3

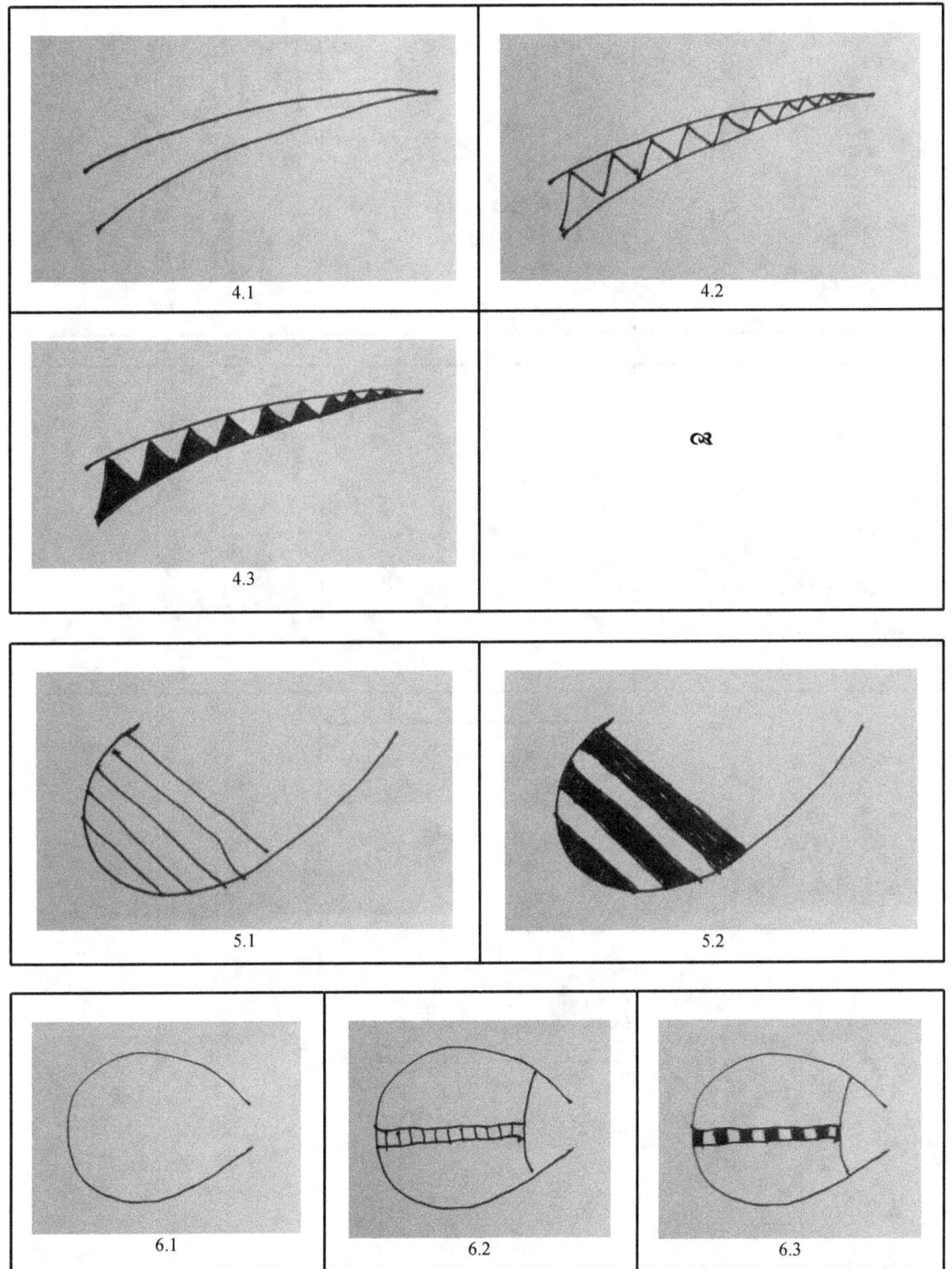

4.1

4.2

4.3

℘

5.1

5.2

6.1

6.2

6.3

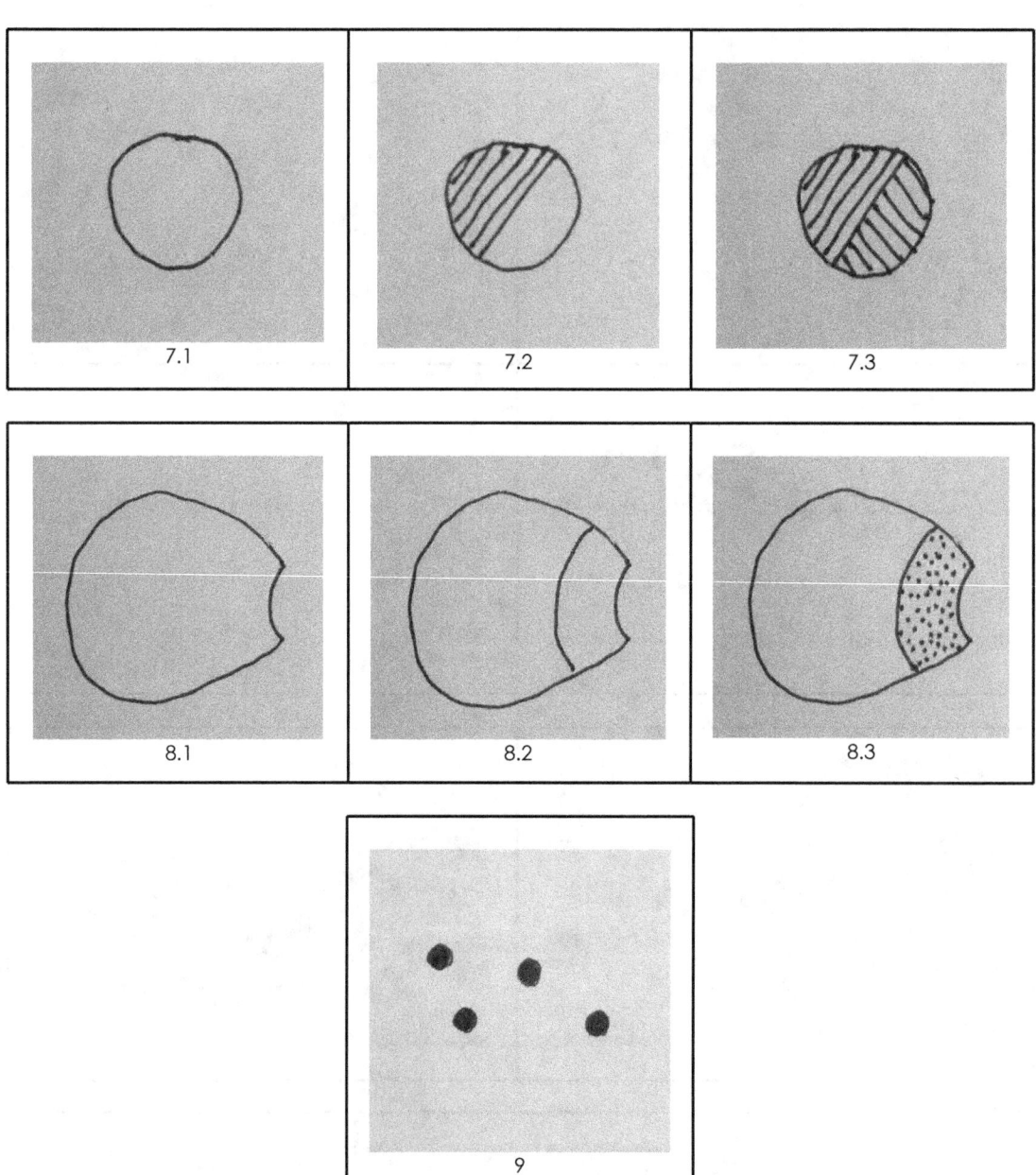

7.1 7.2 7.3

8.1 8.2 8.3

9

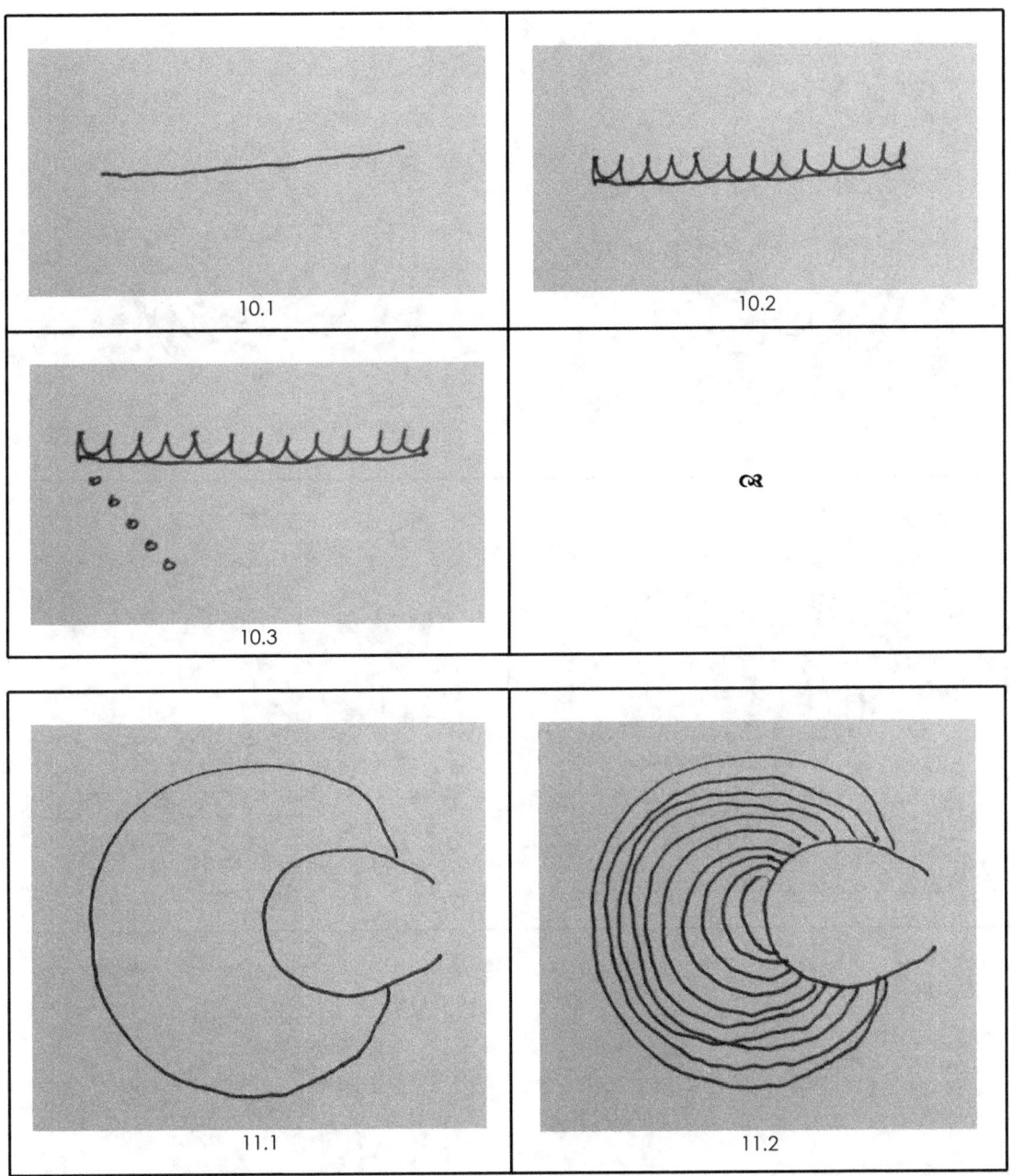

10.1

10.2

10.3

℃

11.1

11.2

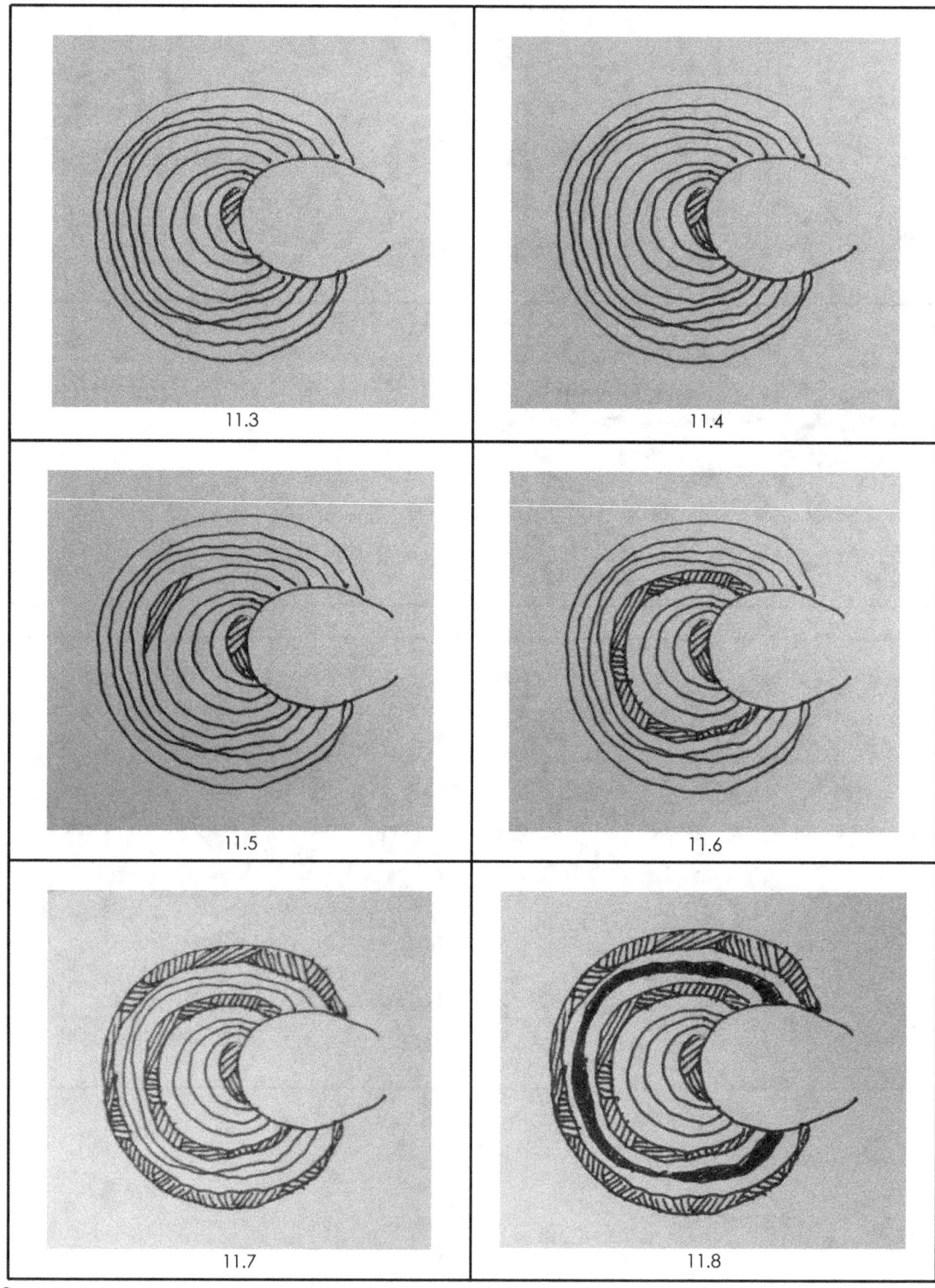

11.3

11.4

11.5

11.6

11.7

11.8

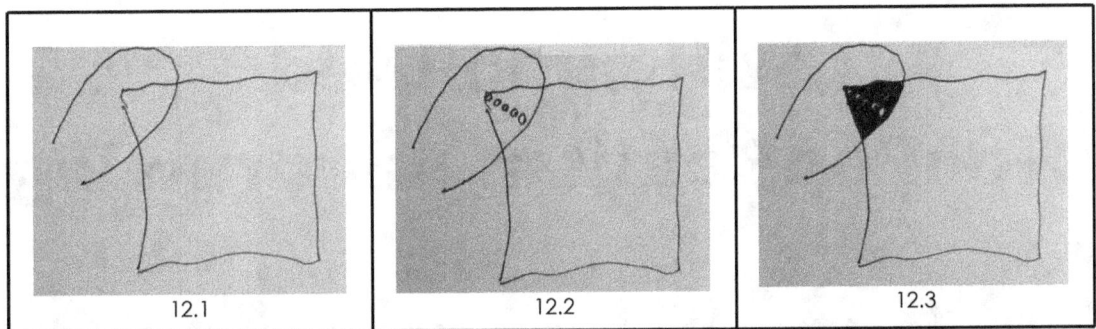

12.1   12.2   12.3

How to create advanced but still simplified NeoPopRealism ink drawing

The following pages will show step-by-step how to create advanced, but still simplified NeoPopRealism ink drawing "*Two Faces*". To create this drawing you need artistic talent and some skills. Every following image includes new additional details. This is how the final drawing looks:

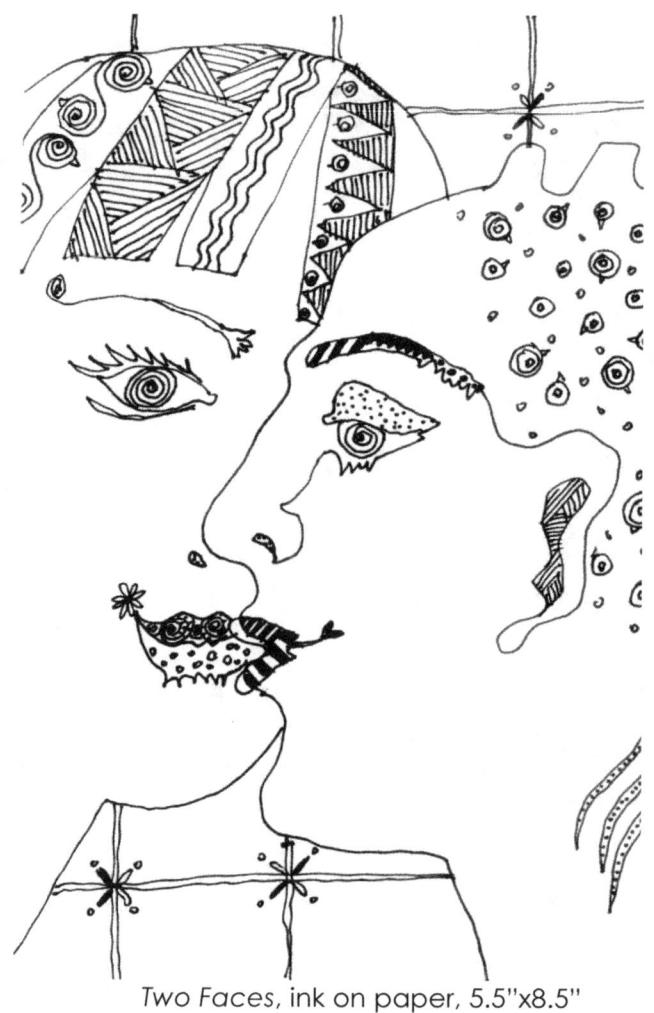

Two Faces, ink on paper, 5.5"x8.5"

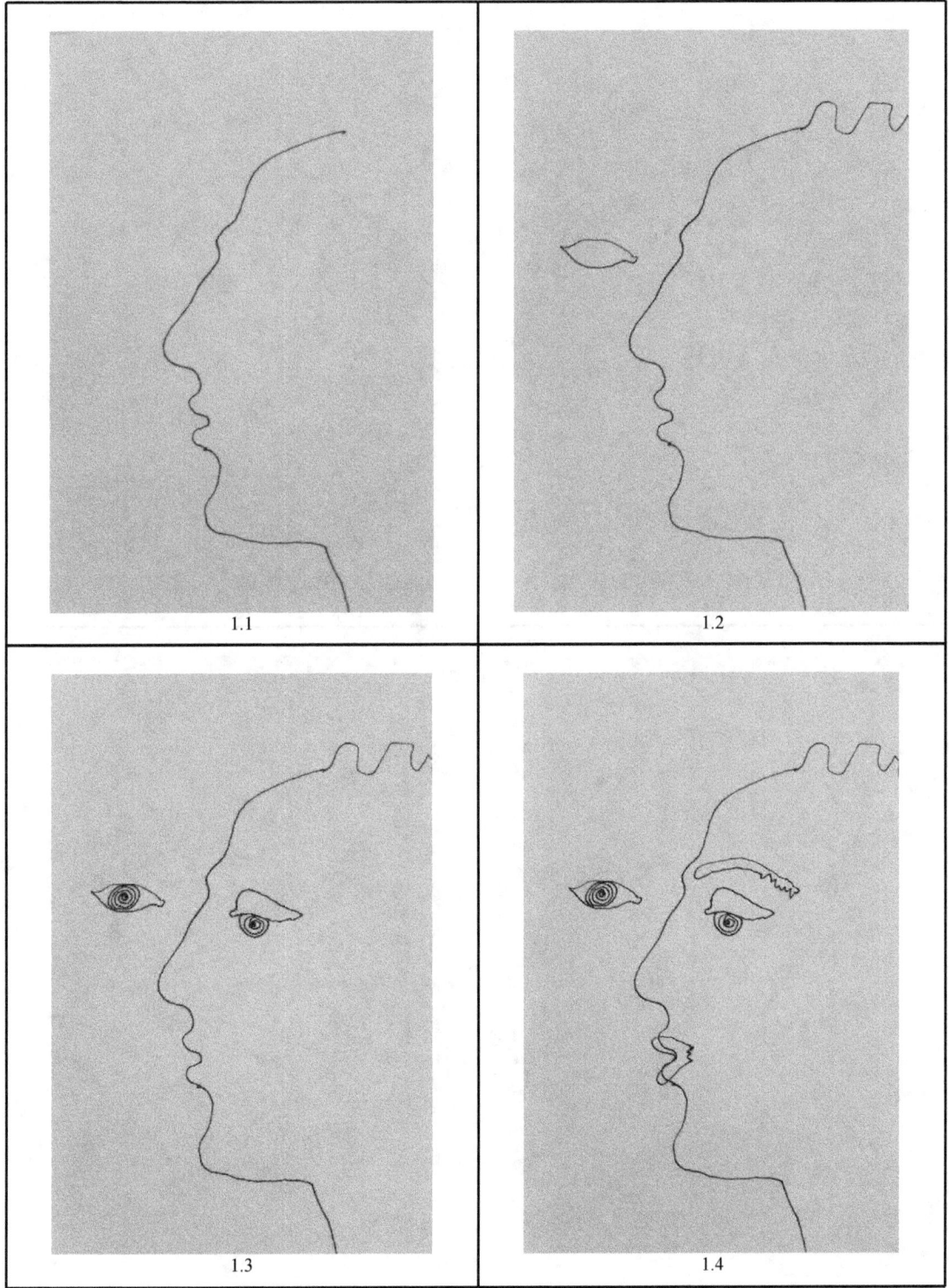

1.1

1.2

1.3

1.4

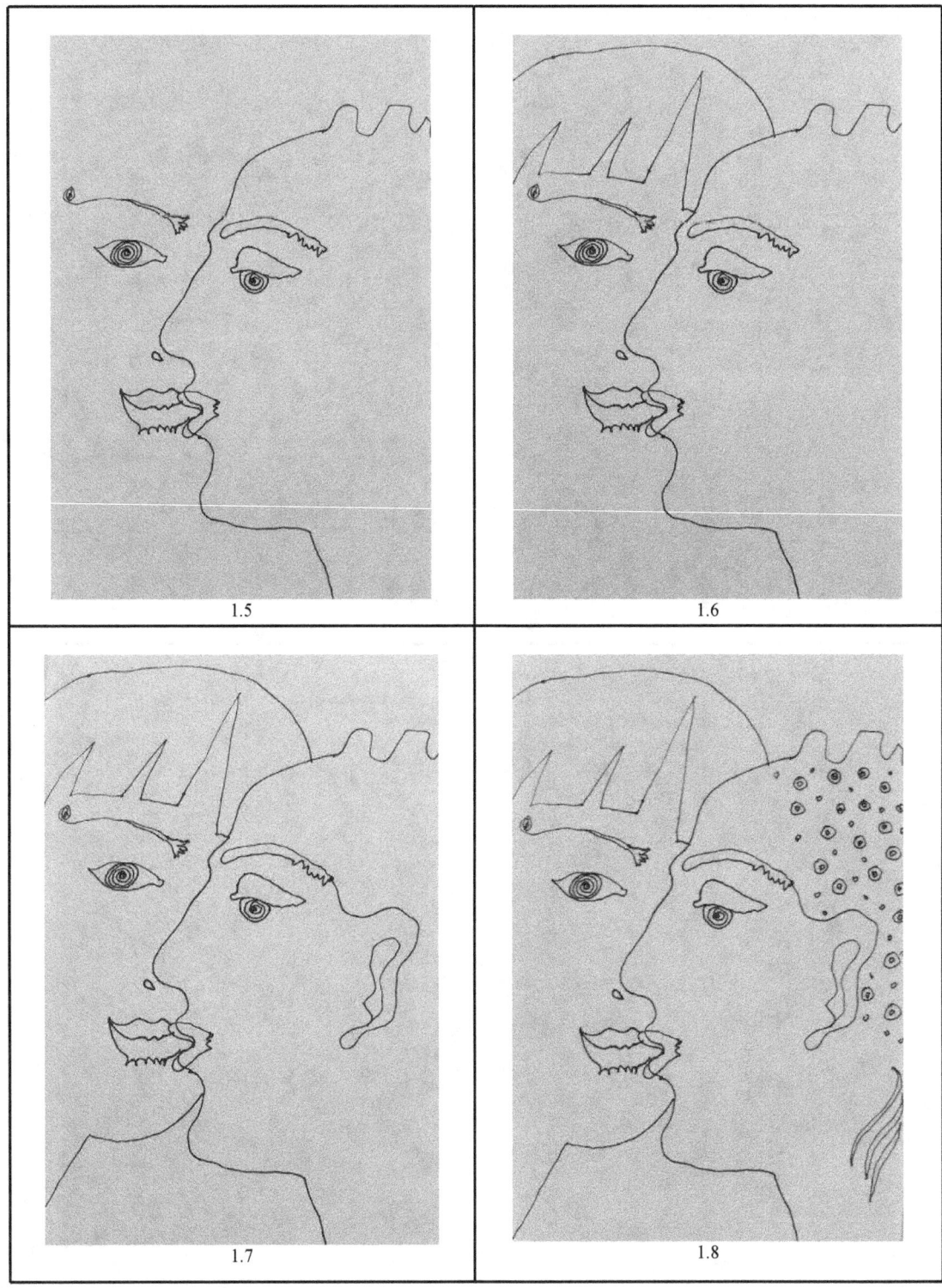

1.5

1.6

1.7

1.8

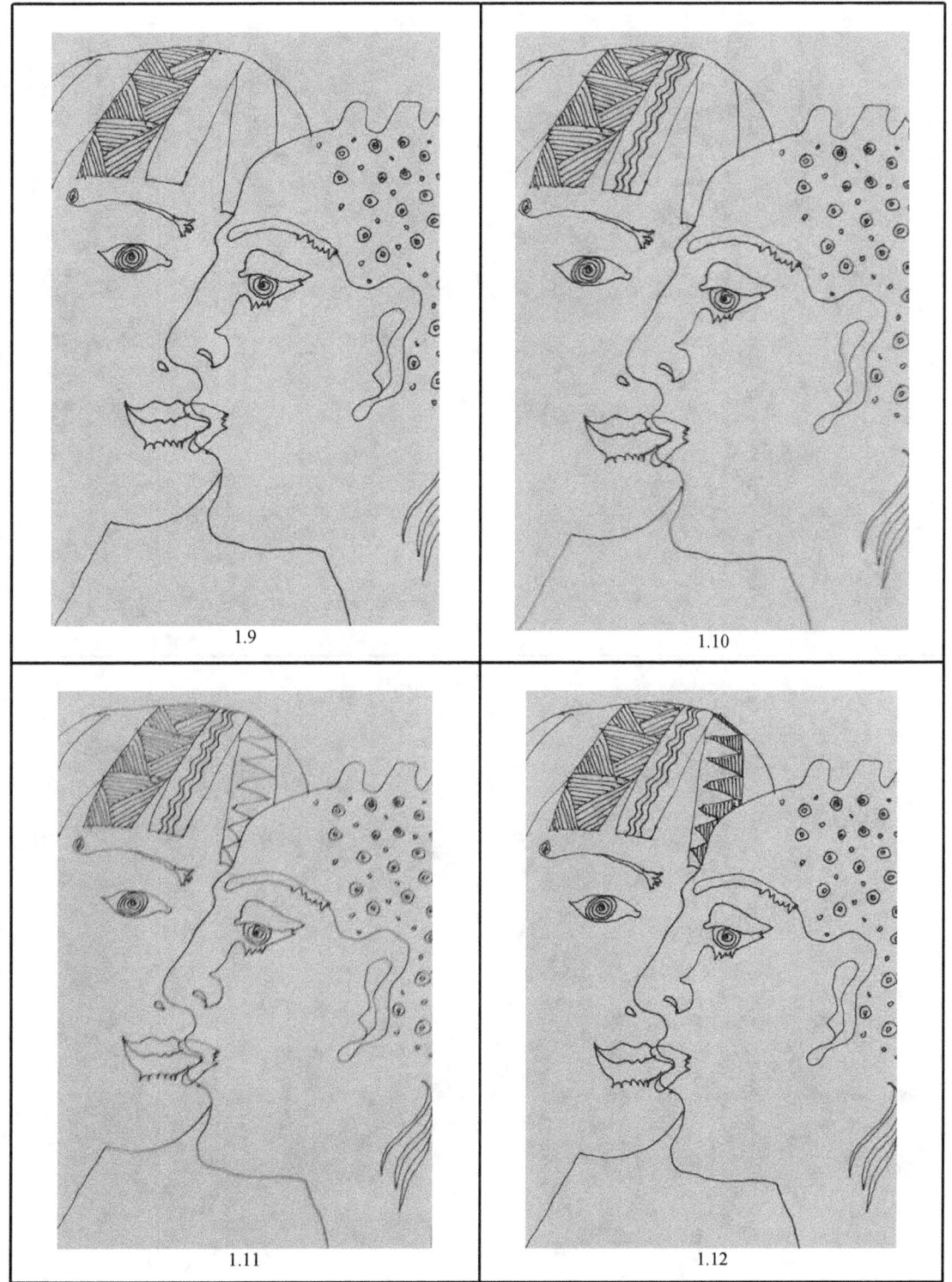

1.9

1.10

1.11

1.12

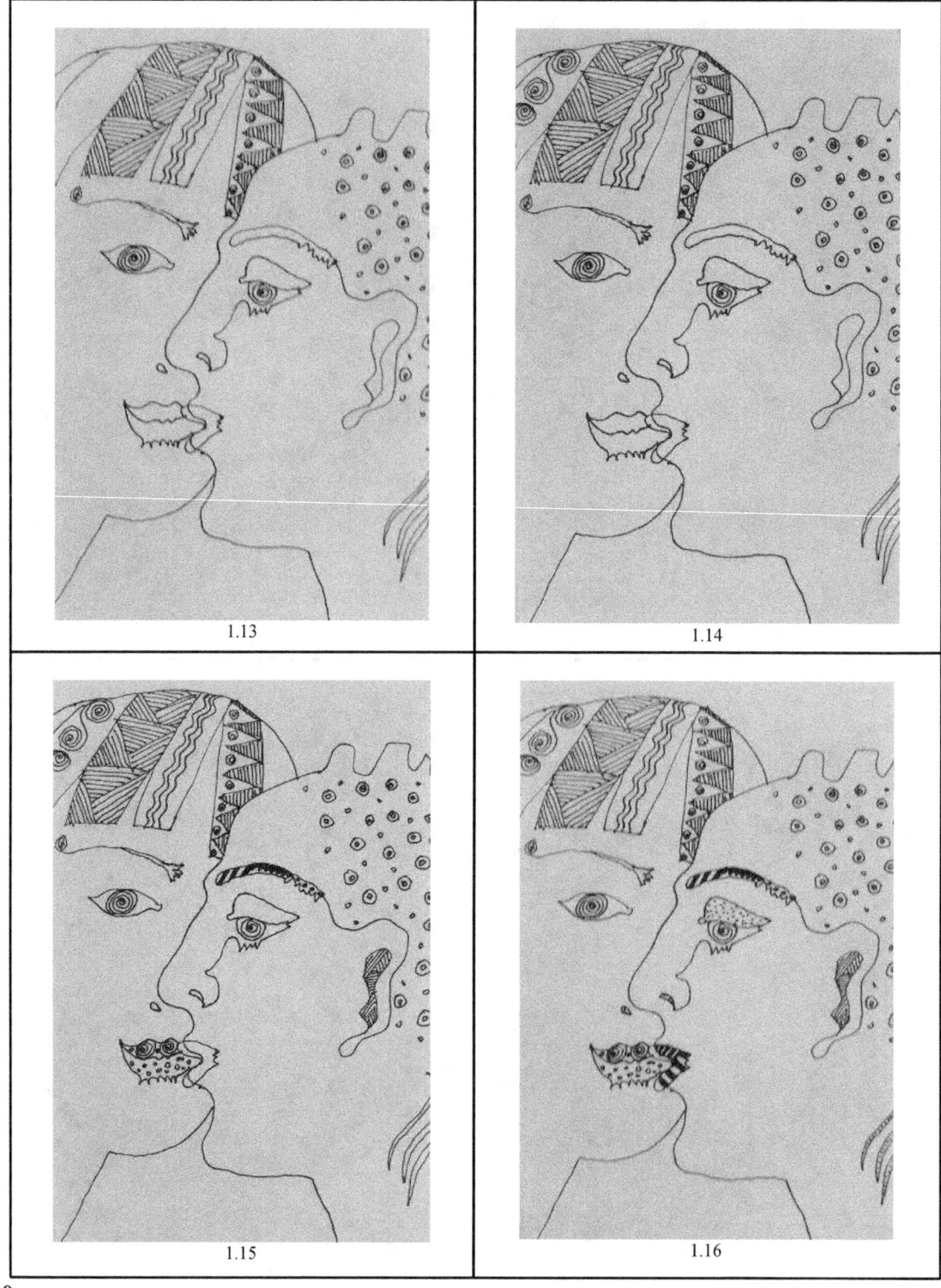

1.13

1.14

1.15

1.16

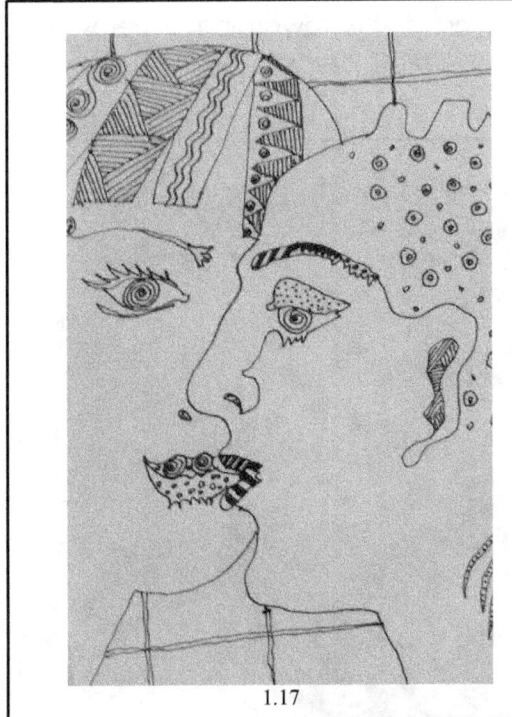

1.17

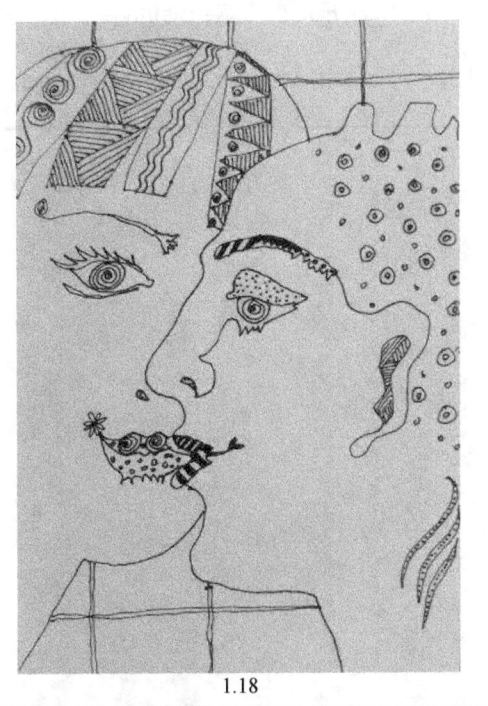

1.18

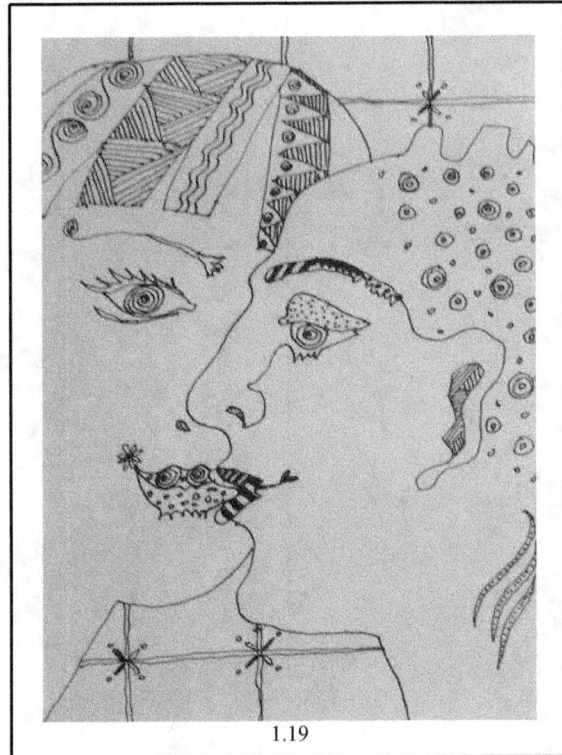

1.19

The following pages show step-by-step how to create repetitive patterns, used in drawing "*Two Faces*." Repetitive patterns' drawing is very rewarding; it helps you to experience calm, ease, and peace of mind, increasing your energy and vitality and regulate your natural healing hormones.

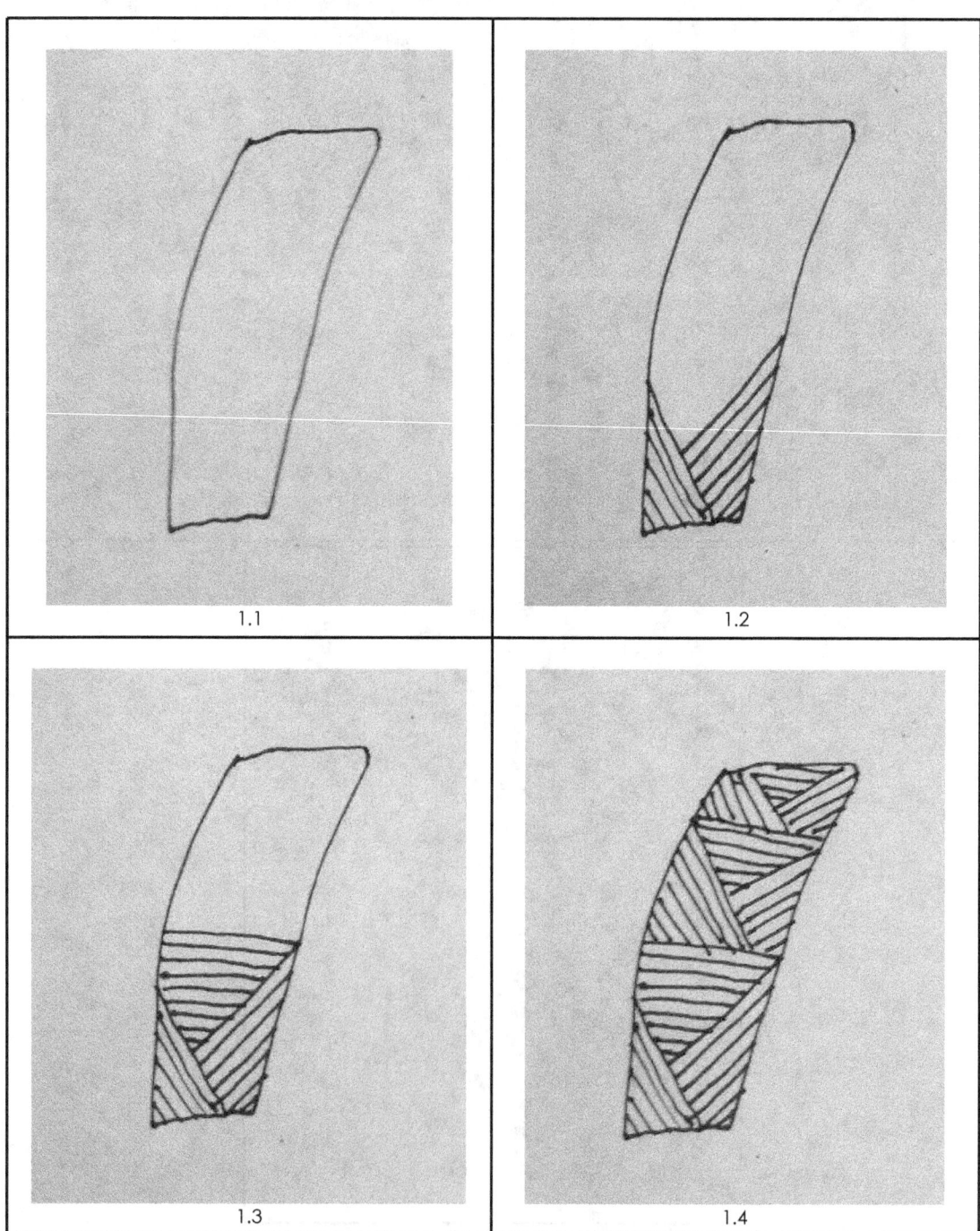

1.1

1.2

1.3

1.4

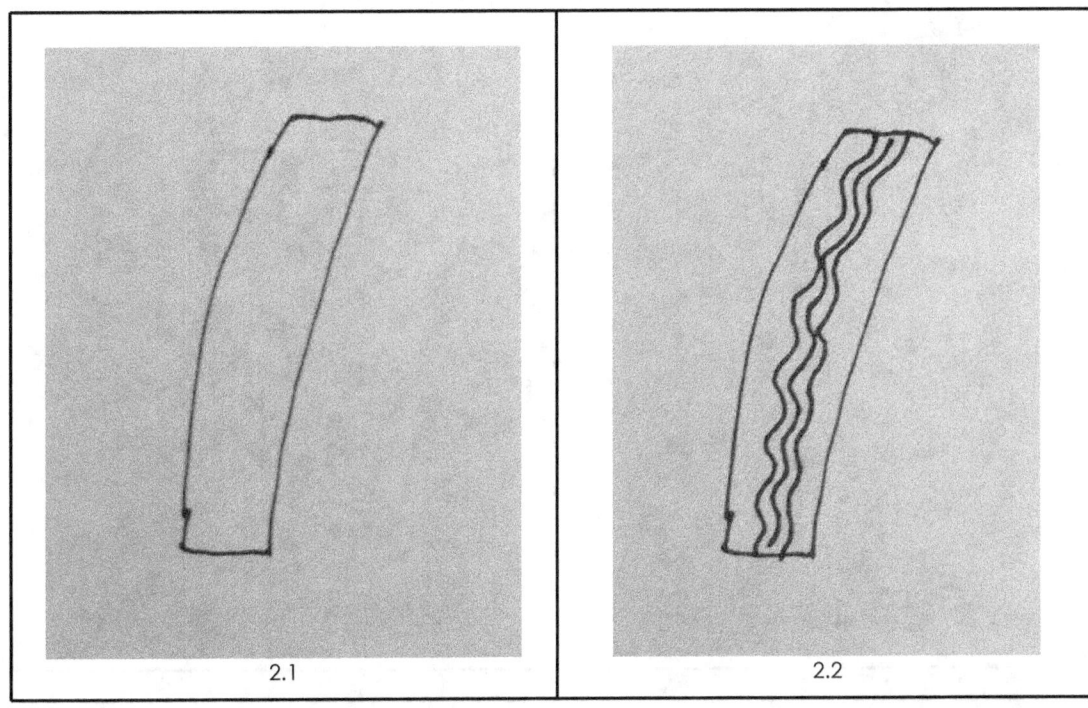

2.1

2.2

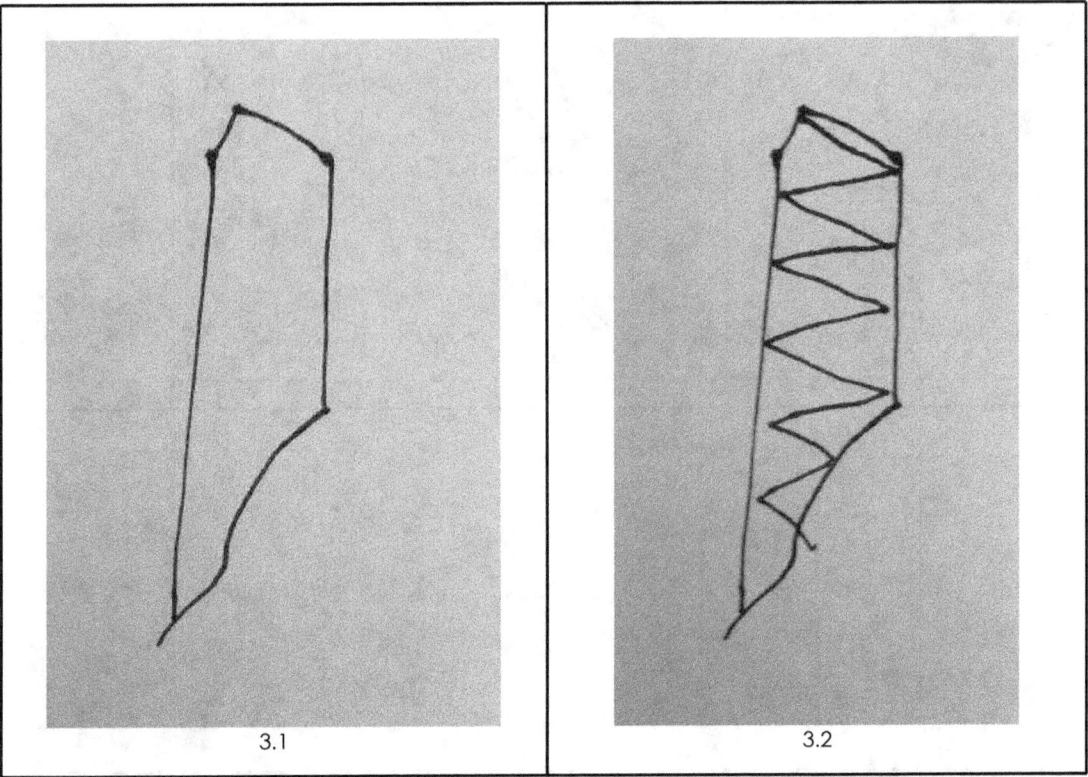

3.1

3.2

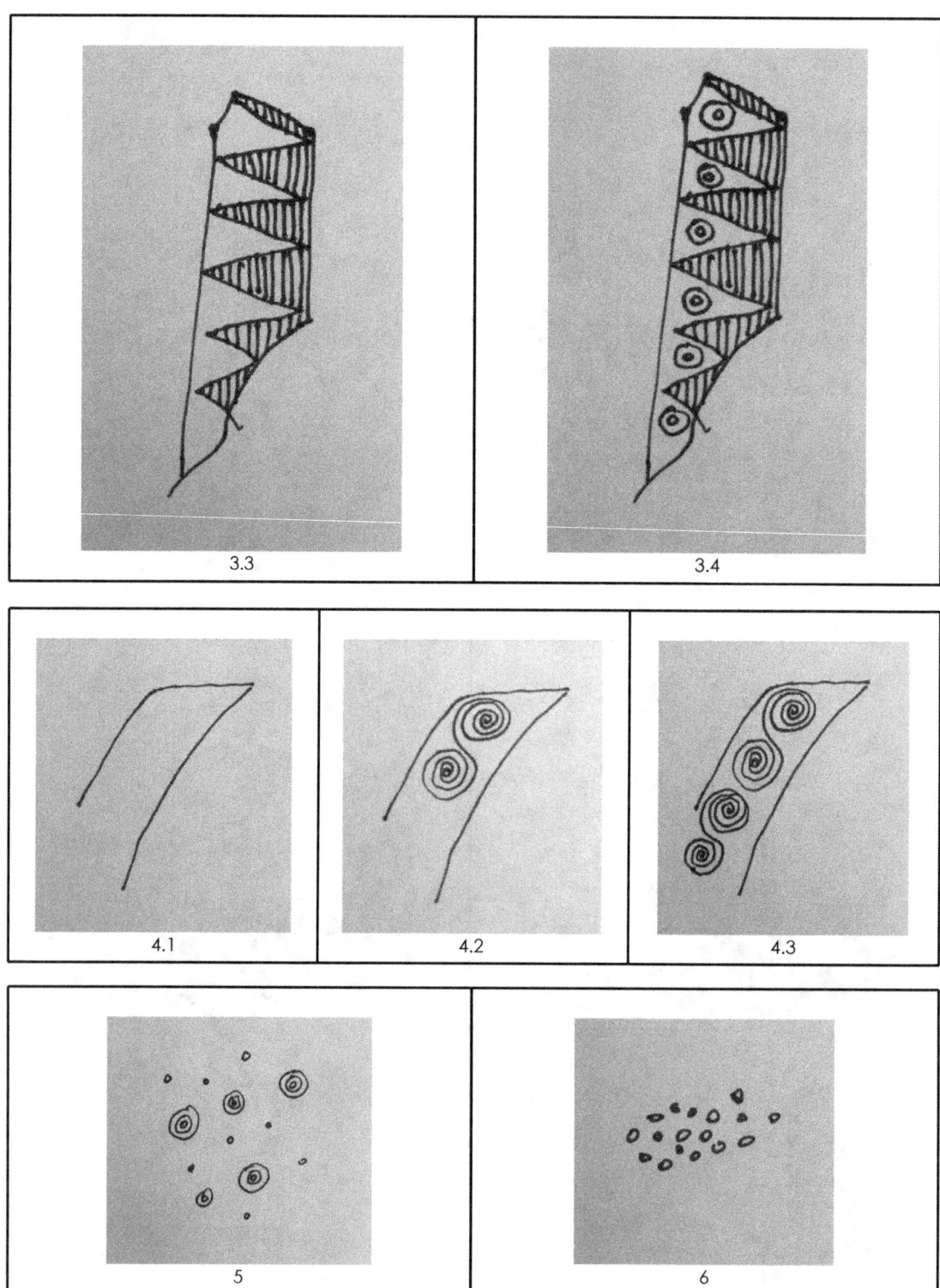

3.3

3.4

4.1

4.2

4.3

5

6

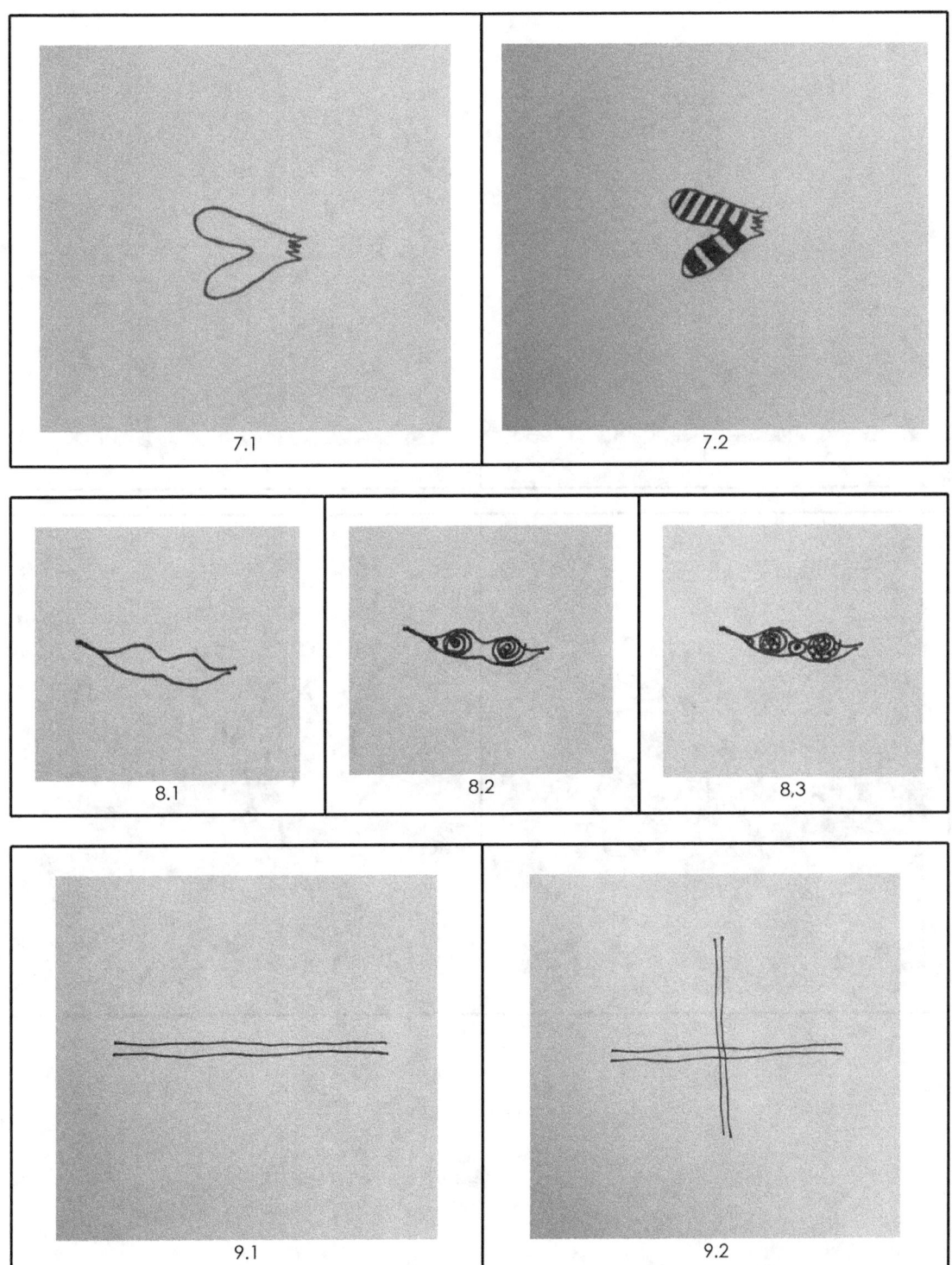

7.1

7.2

8.1

8.2

8,3

9.1

9.2

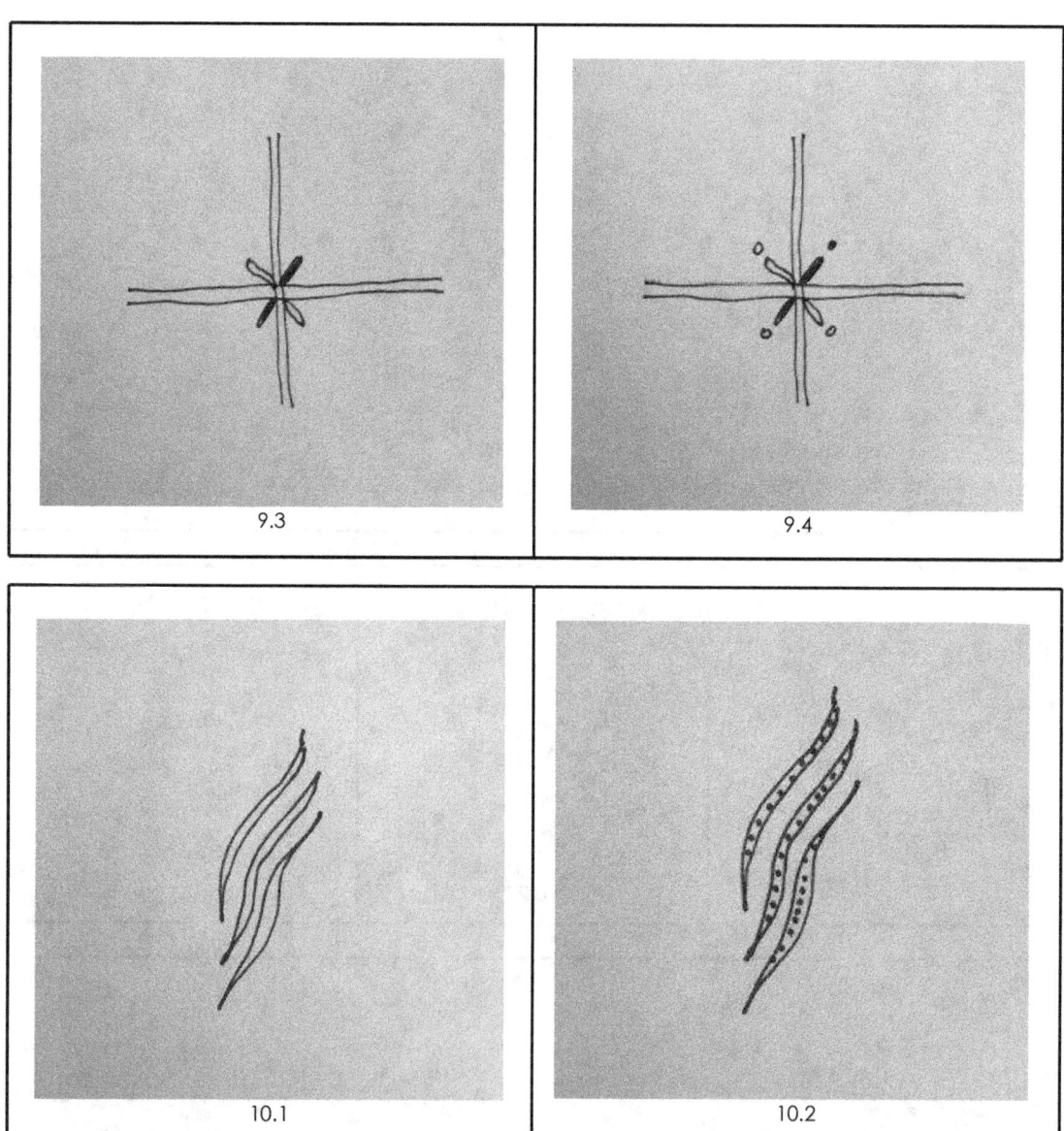

9.3

9.4

10.1

10.2

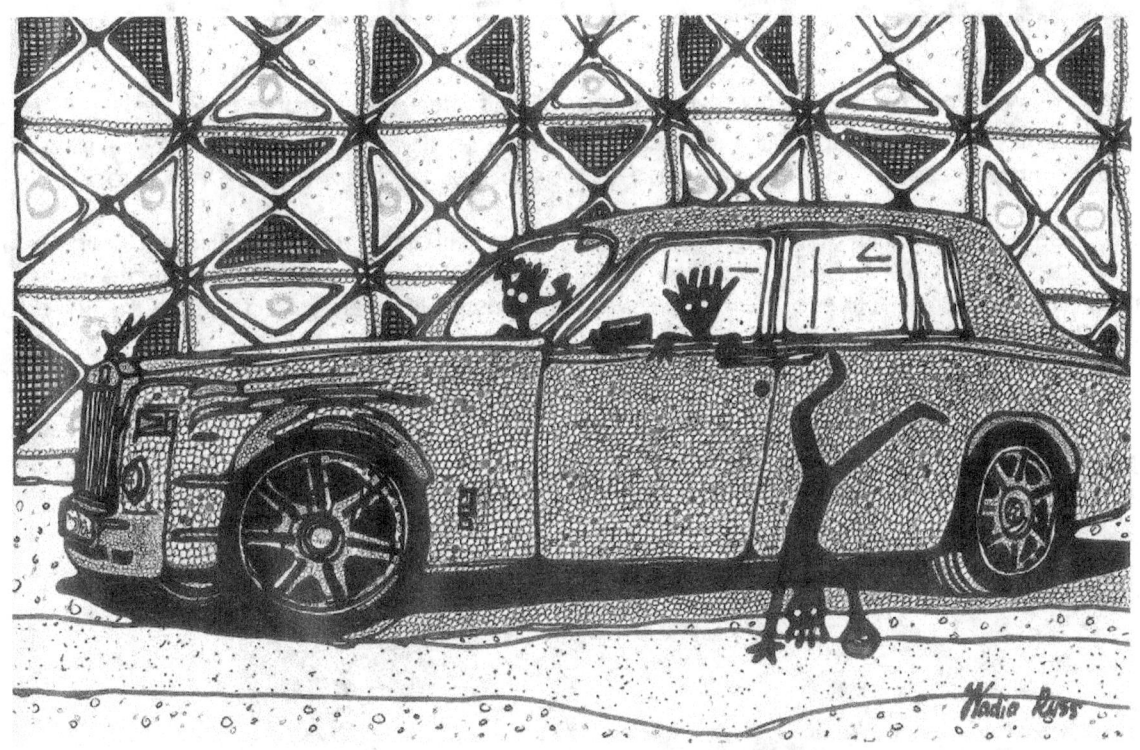

Nadia Russ, *Rolls Royce D'Vinci*", ink on paper, 11"x17", 2006

Draw repetitive patterns here and now

The following pages invite you to draw repetitive patterns here and now, develop your artistic skills. All you need is a thin ink pen, because thick ink pen will leave marks on another side of page. Open your mind to possibilities and remember that impossible is nothing.

Our world is fast and challenging, fun and demanding, exciting and frightening. It produces emotional reactions, stress, worry and anxiety, but we can tolerate only so much of it. The repetitive patterns' drawing process will open you doors to the level of meditation and relaxation you never experienced before. Practice daily and you will discover new you, with wide eyes open to the new opportunities in visual arts and in life in general.

Complete each section with the offered repetitive patterns (page 37) and at the end your image will look like this:

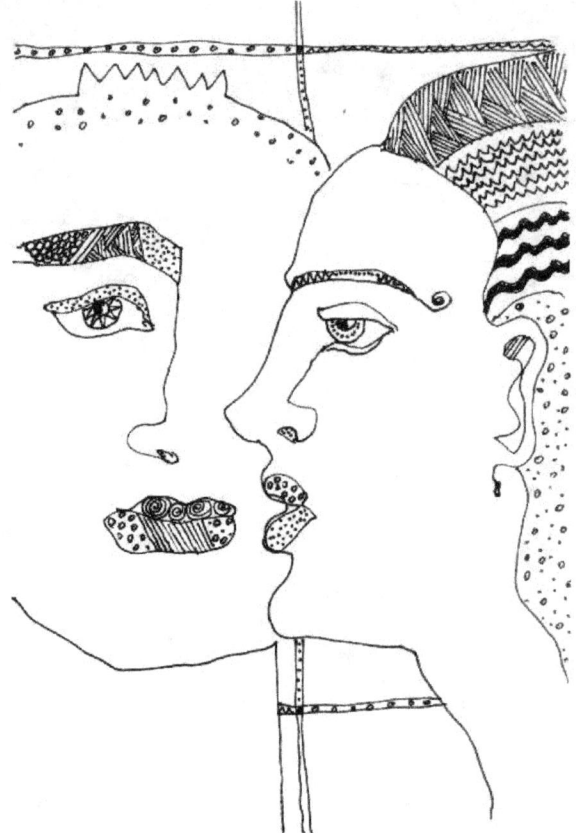

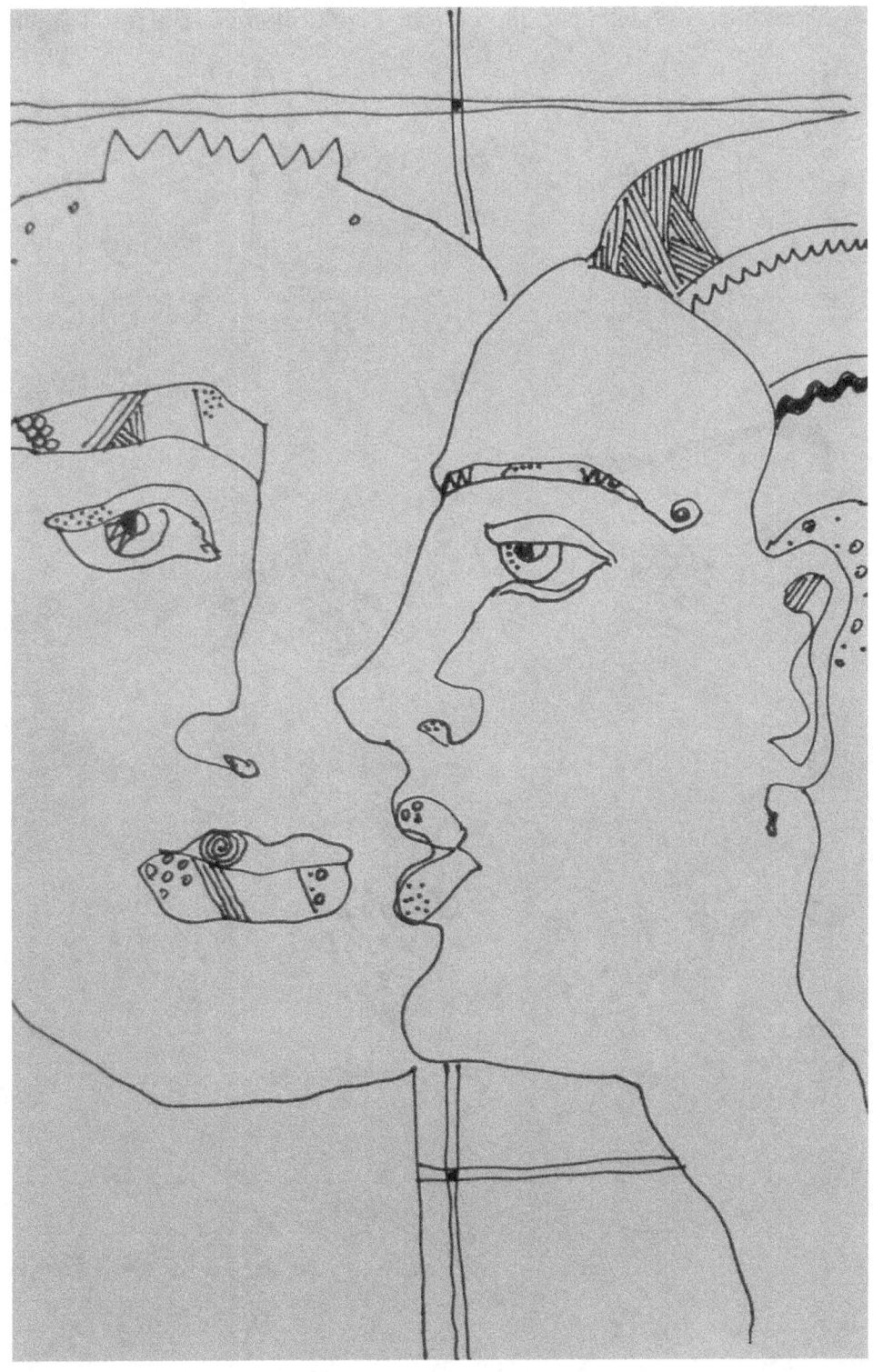

Fill sections (page 39) with the offered repetitive patterns to get result like this:

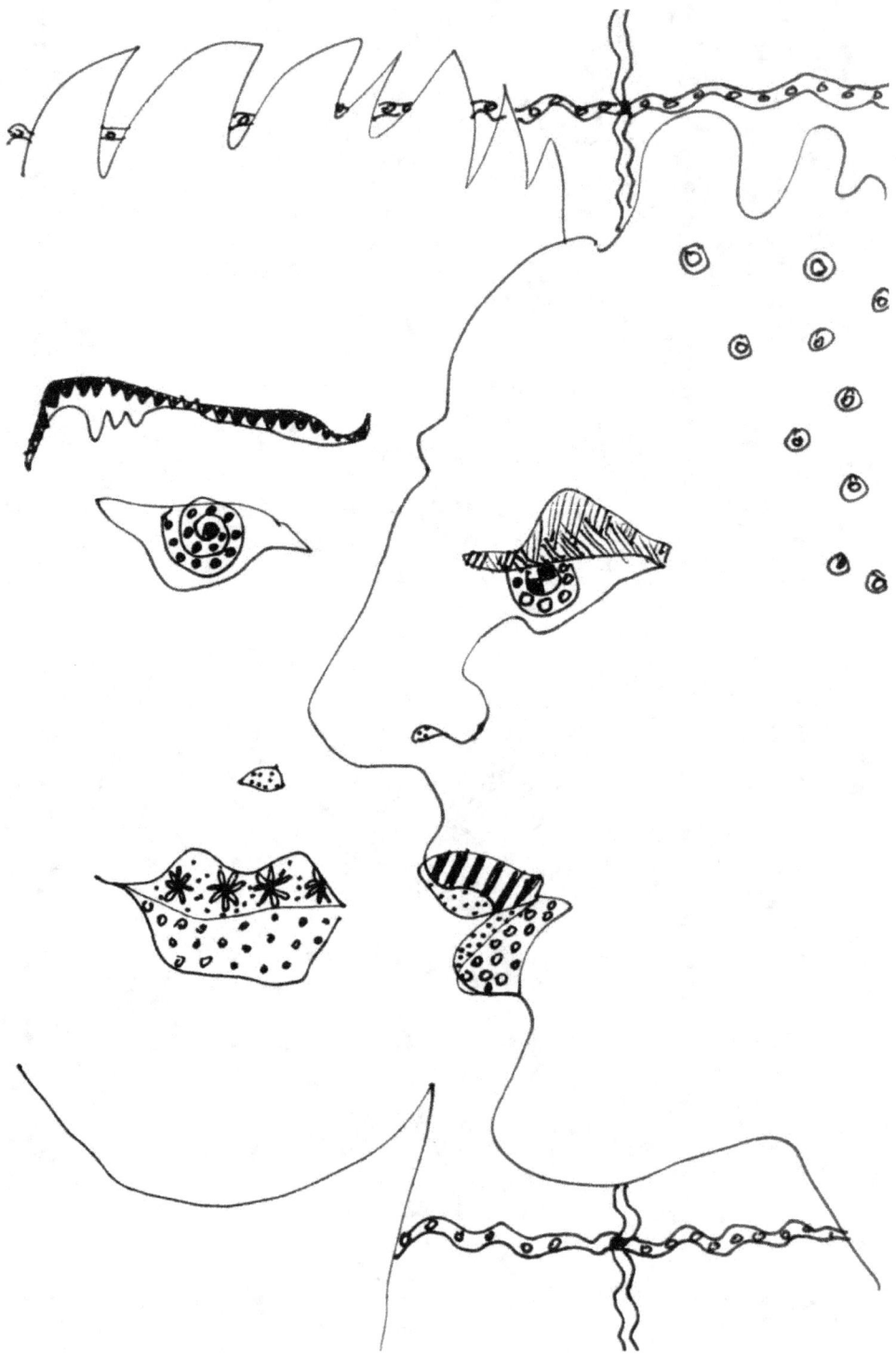

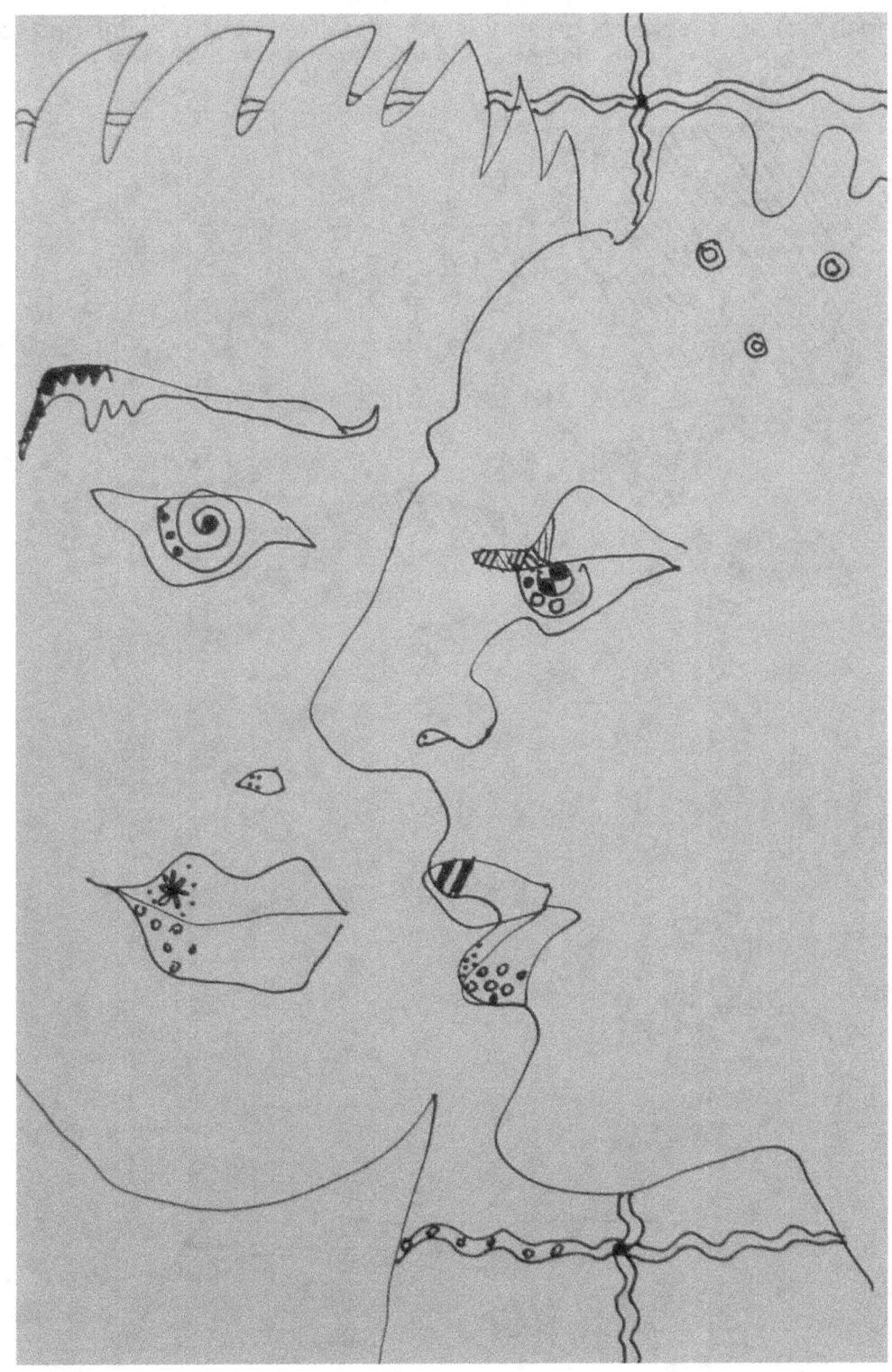

Fill each section of image (page 41) with the offered repetitive patterns, and your image will look like this:

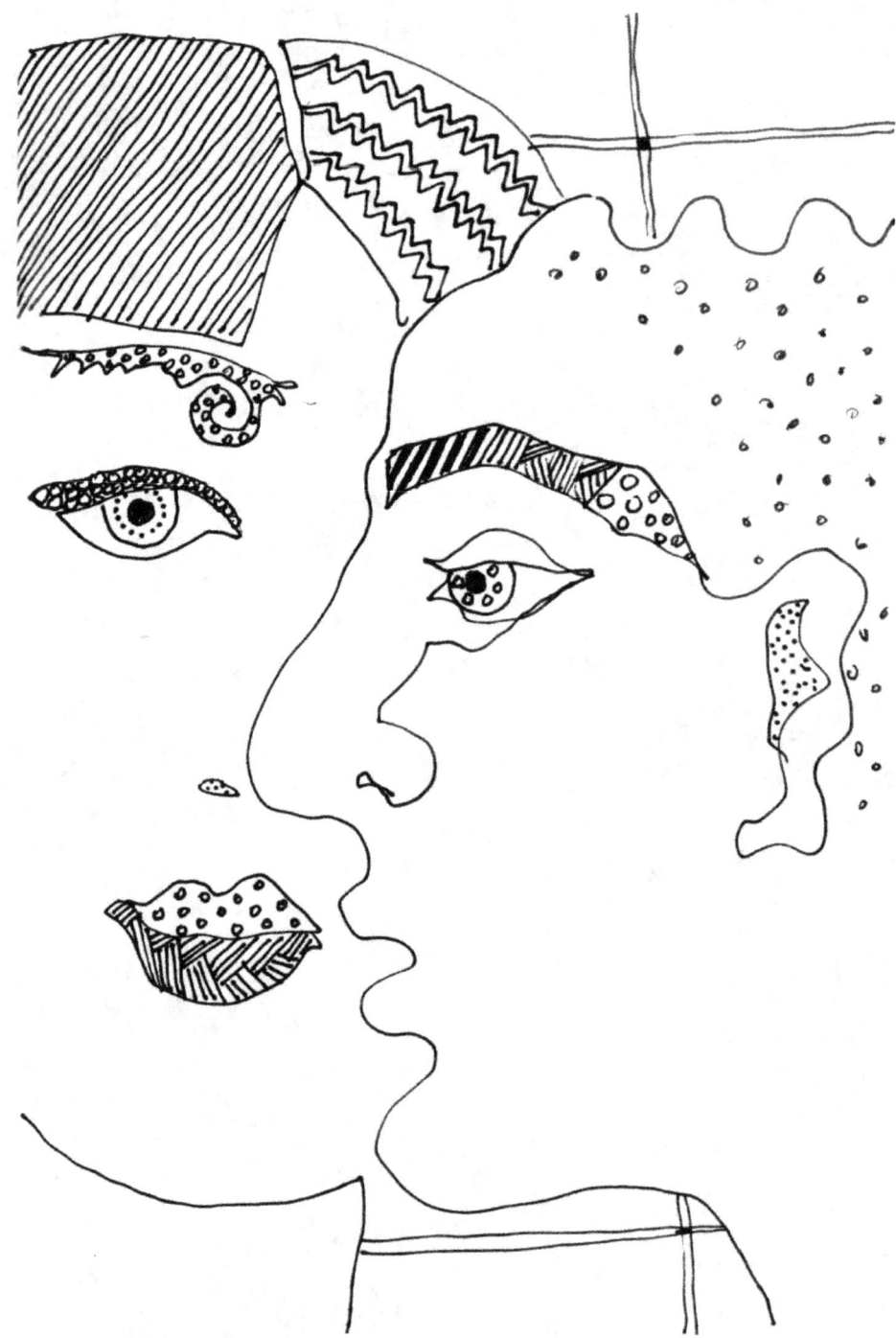

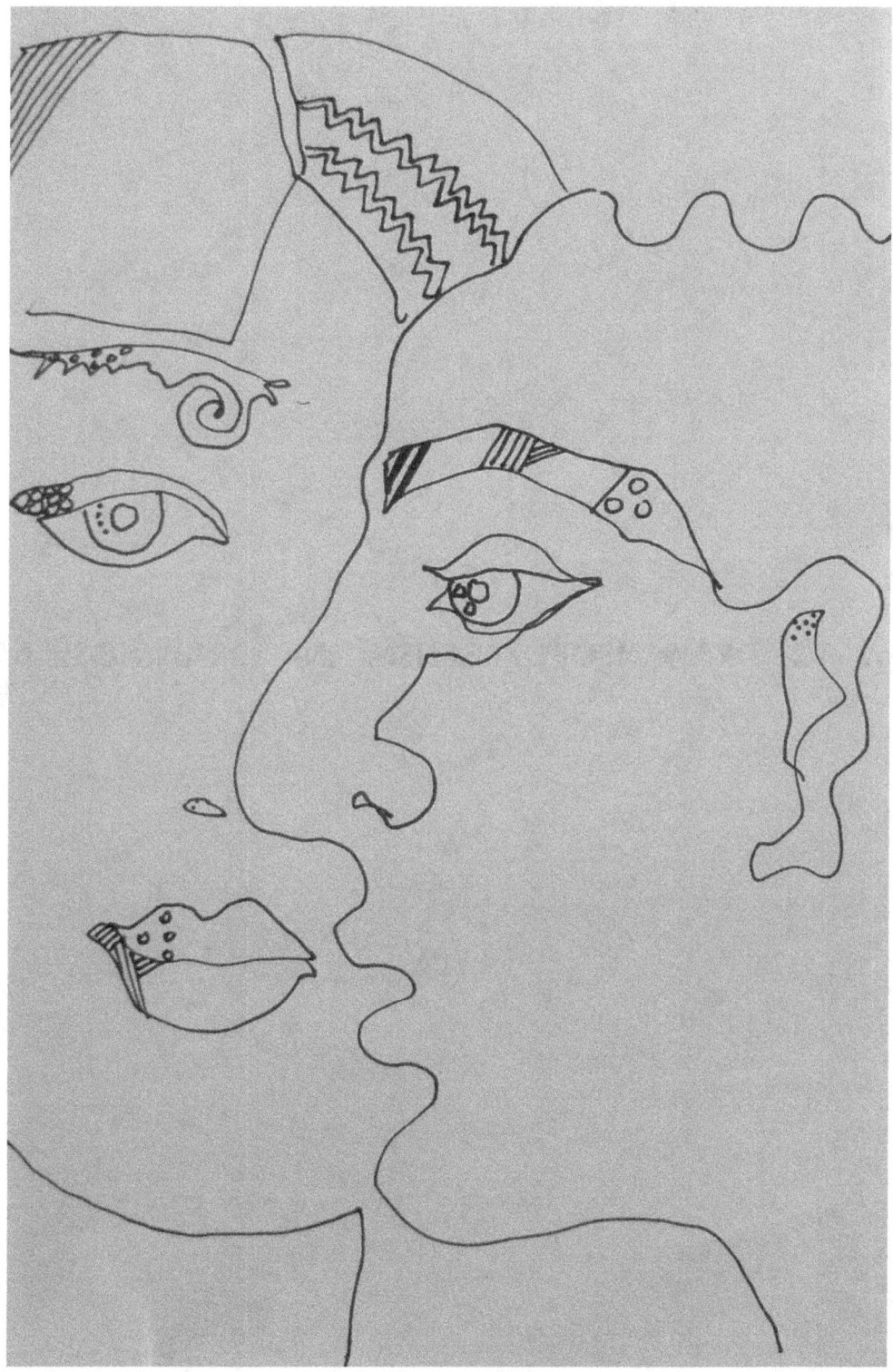

HOW TO DRAW NEOPOPREALISM INK DRAWINGS: BASICS

The following pages (43, 45, 47, 49, 51) give you an opportunity to create repetitive patterns and fill with them sections of each image. Some sections leave without repetitive patterns. Create new repetitive patters using your imagination. Use circles, ovals, triangles, squares, lines; combine them differently.

Focus on what you are doing, try to make it best you can, develop your skills. If you make a "mistake" you need no eraser, because the following repetitive patterns balance the whole compositions and make your "mistake" invisible.

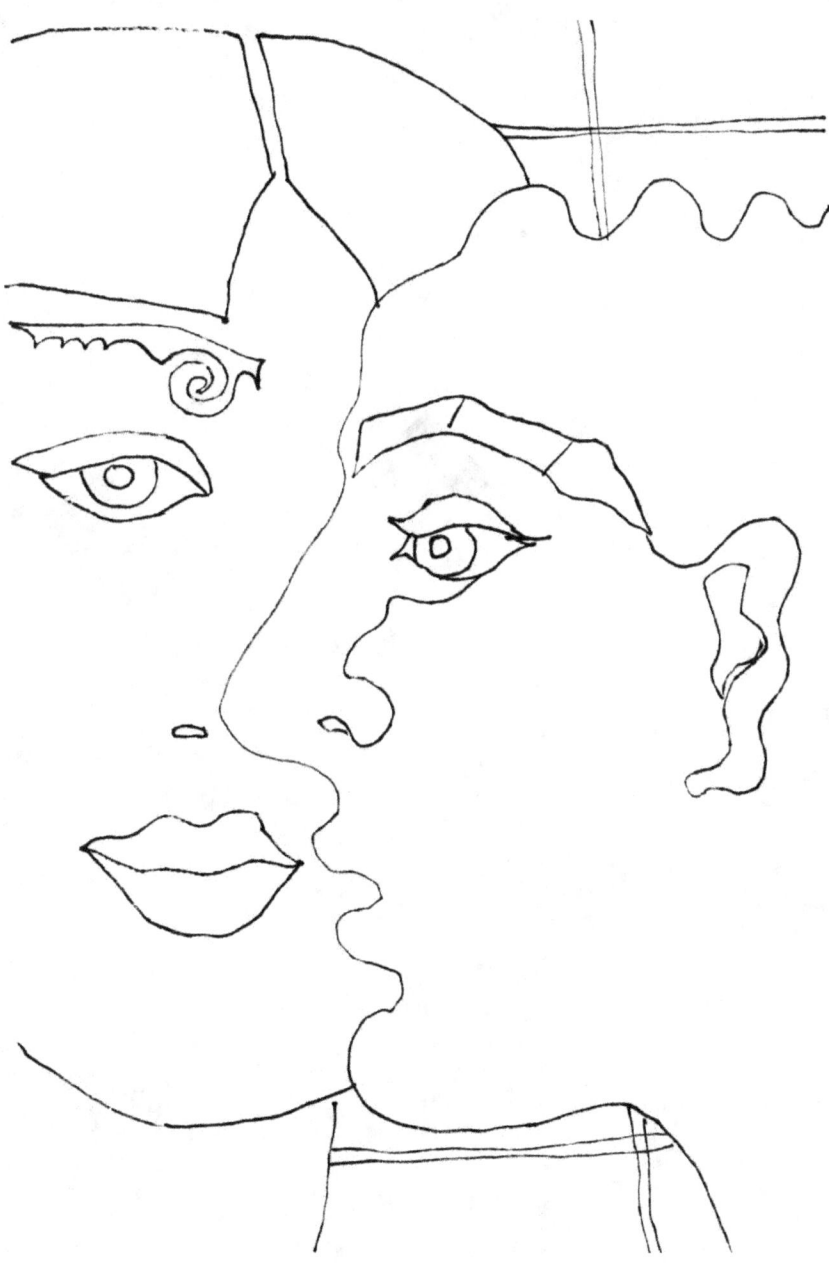

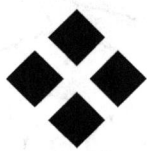

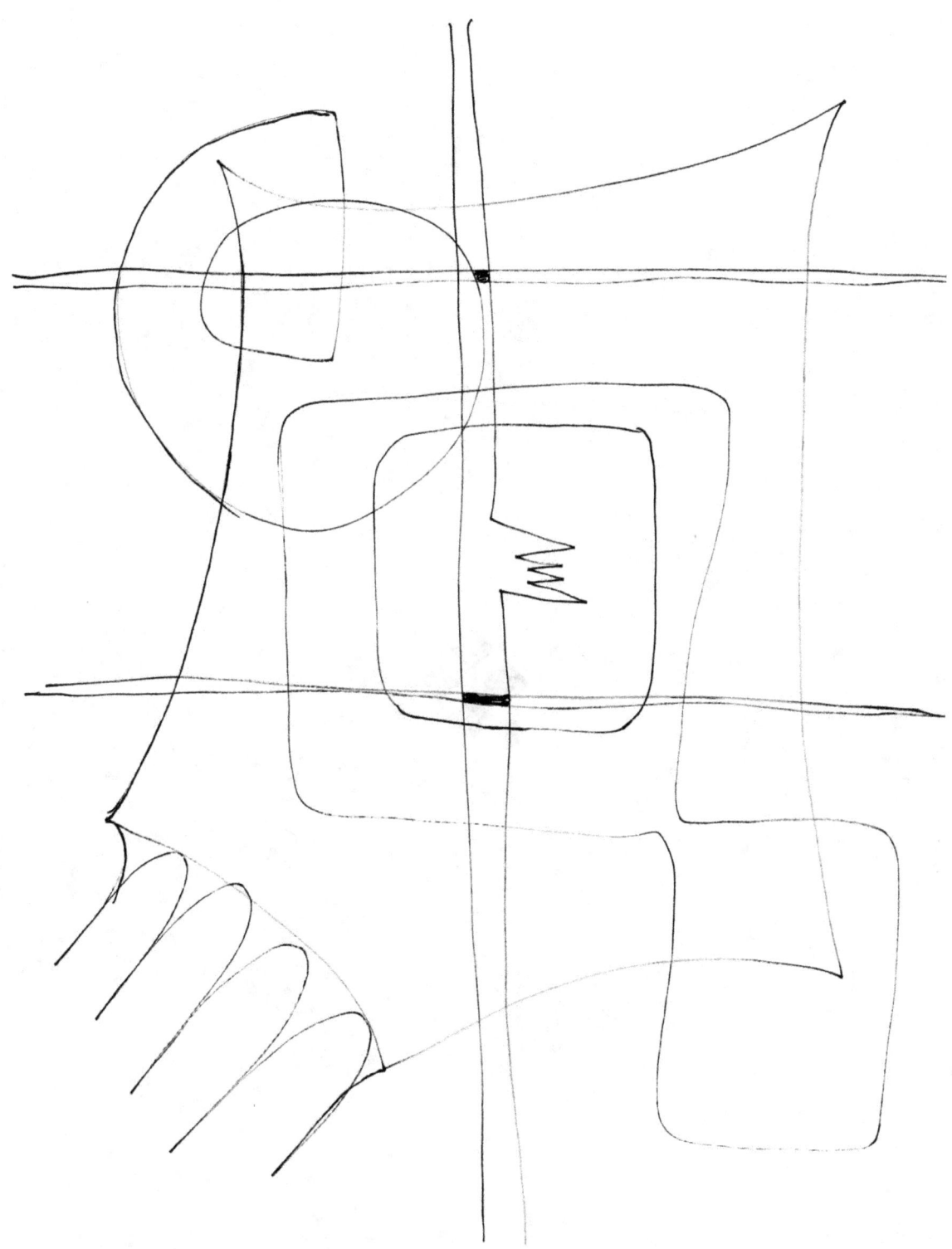

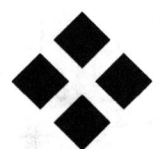

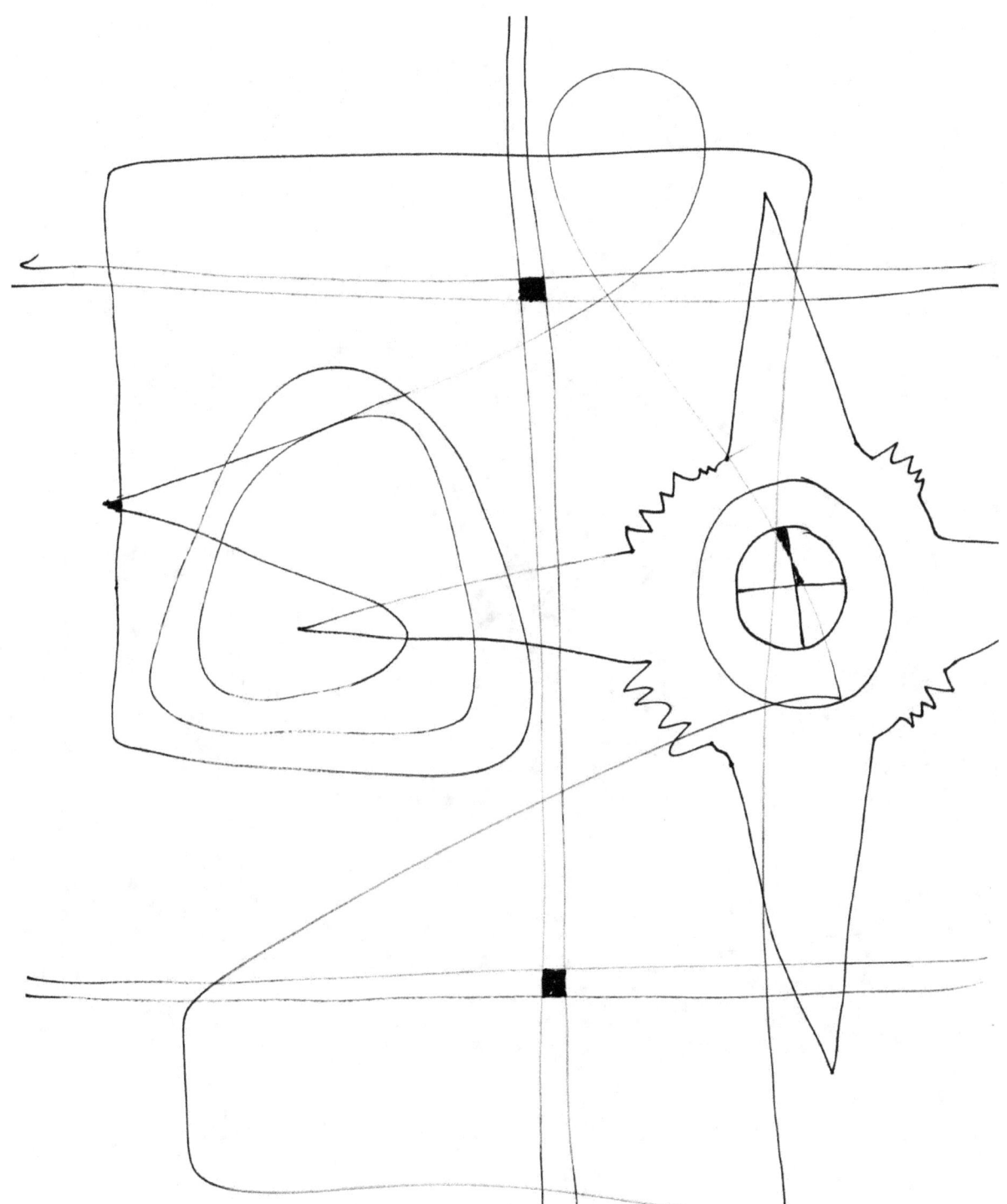

47

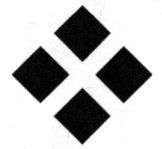

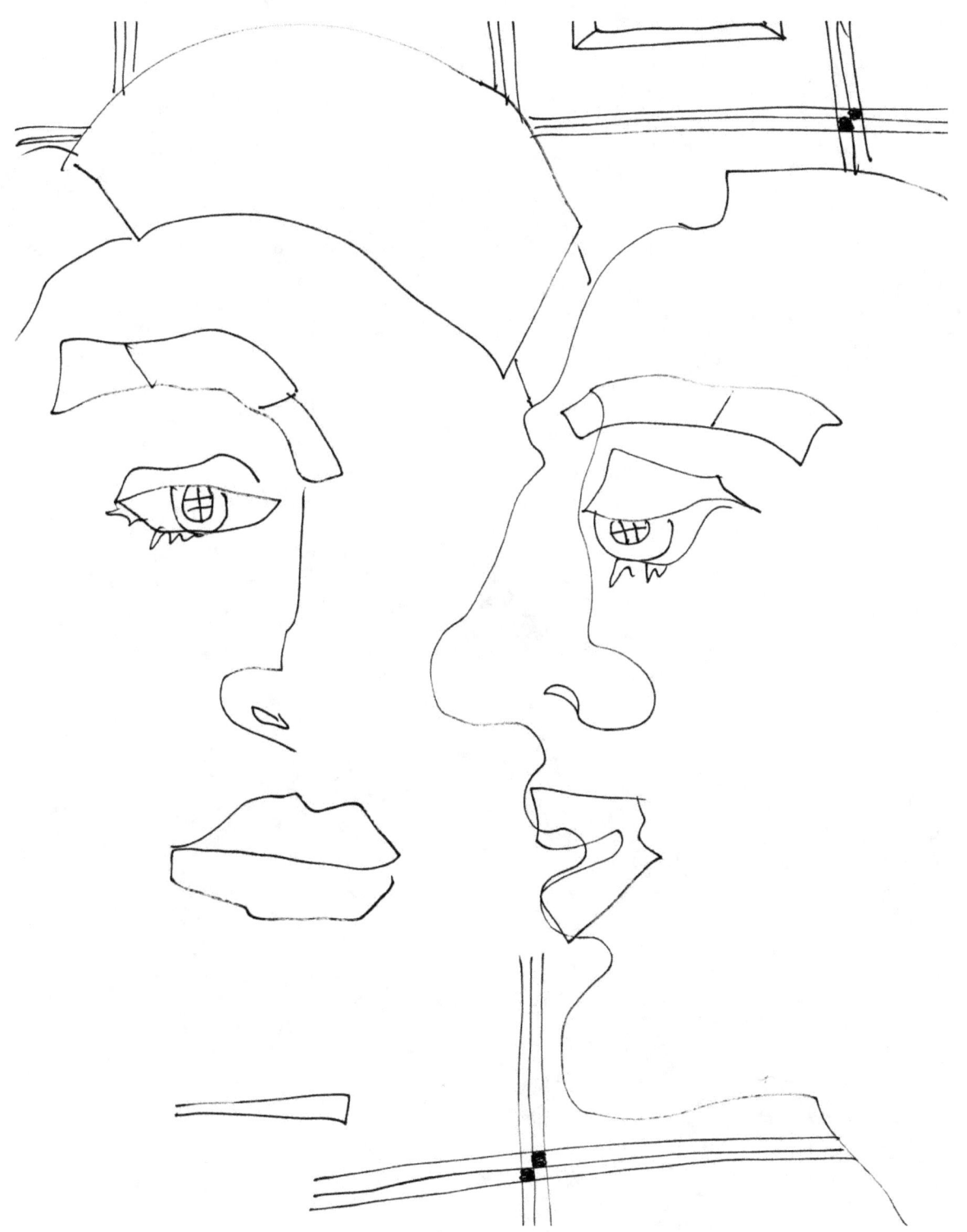

49

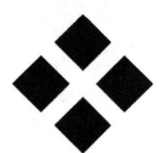

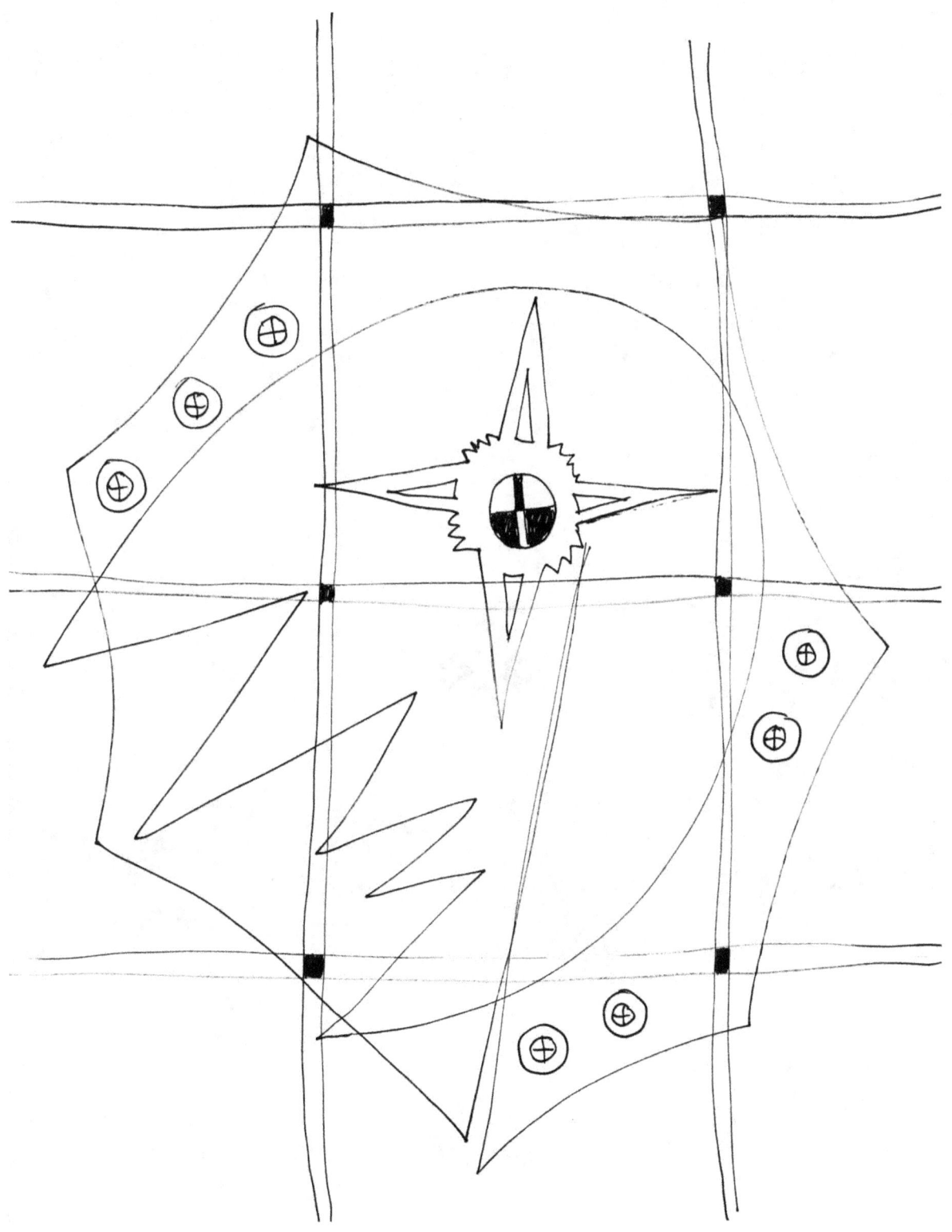

51

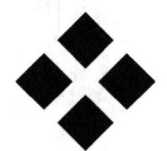

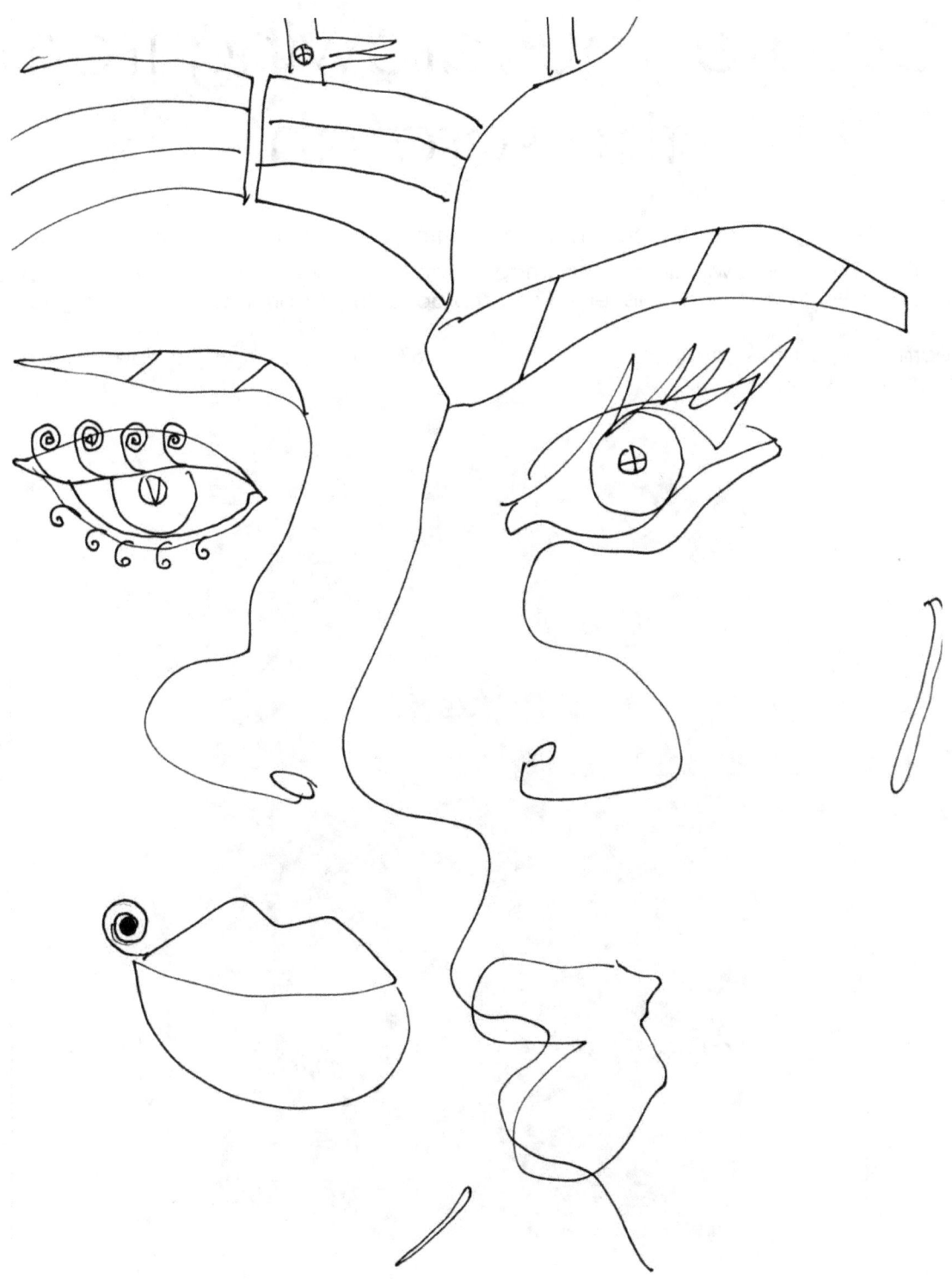

53

Create your drawing from the scratch

The following pages will show how to create your NeoPopRealist drawing from the scratch. Later, you will draw your images with ease, your line will flow without any breaking. But to achieve this level, you must practice and learn how to draw the details.

Learn how to draw the profiles (pages 55, 56, 57). Draw on the right side of the page what you see on the left.

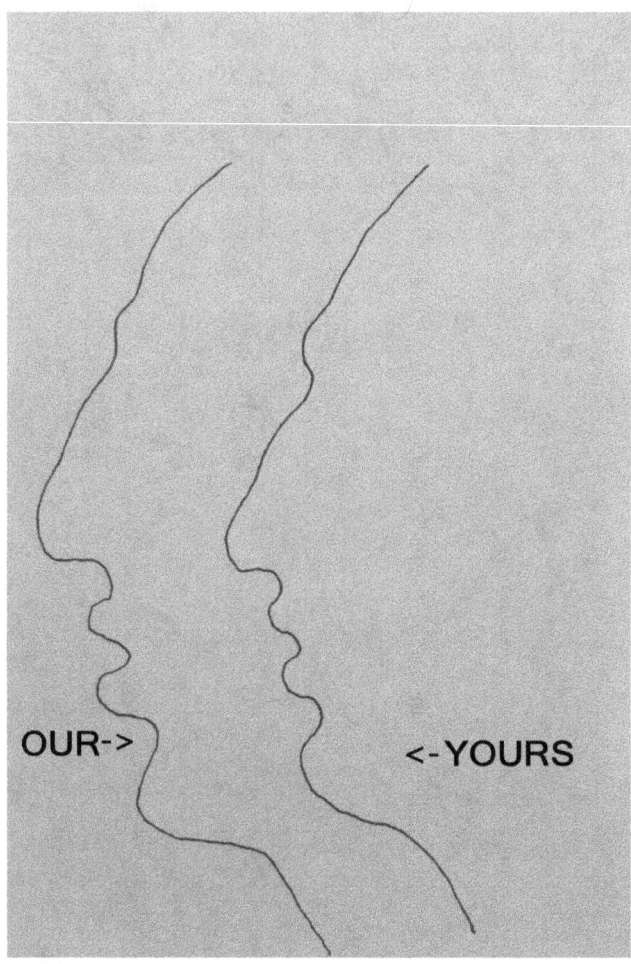

OUR->   <-YOURS

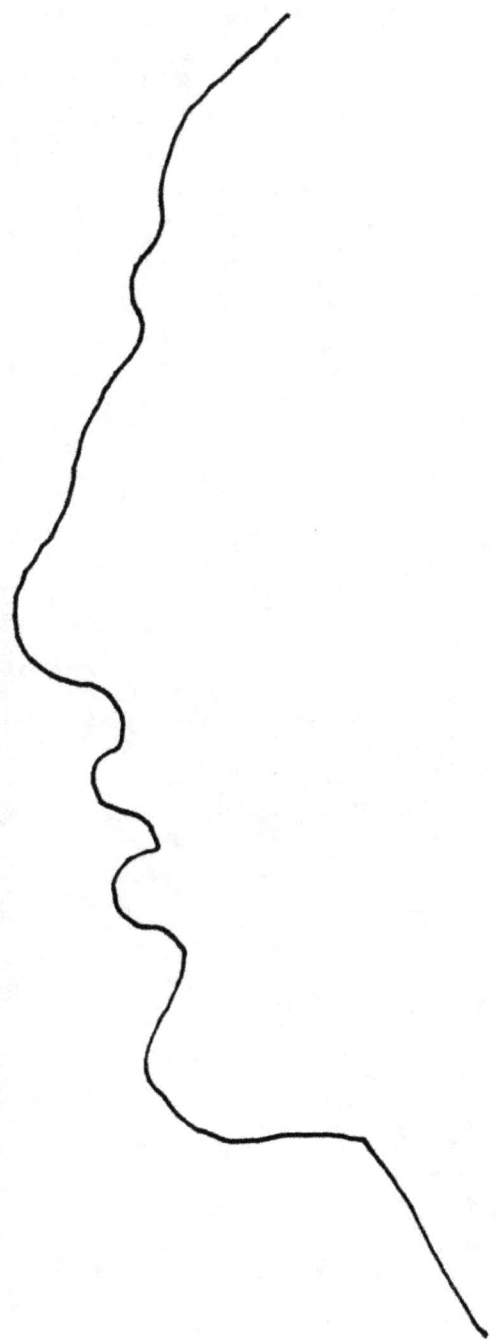

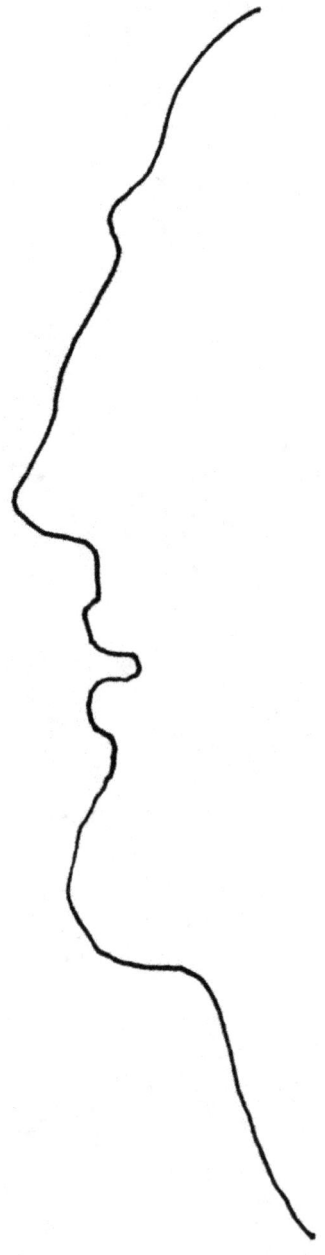

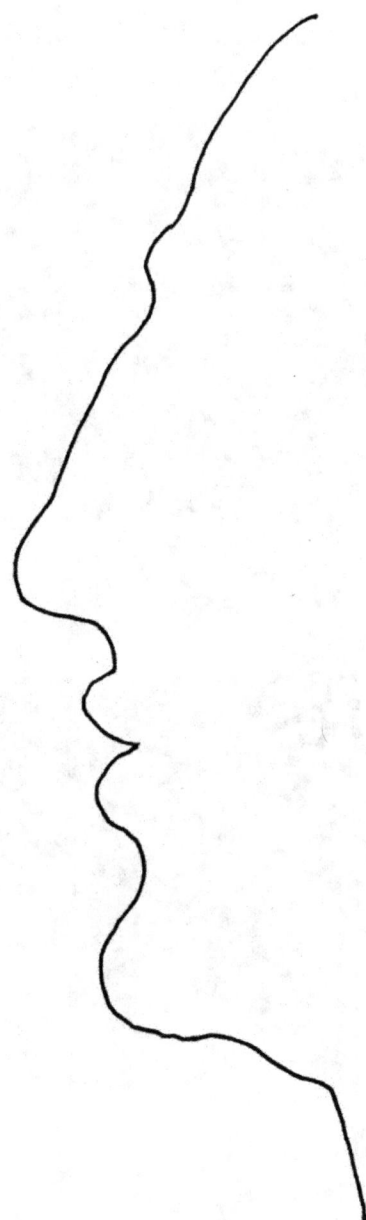

The next pages will show you how to draw the eyes. Draw your eye image on the right as it shown here:

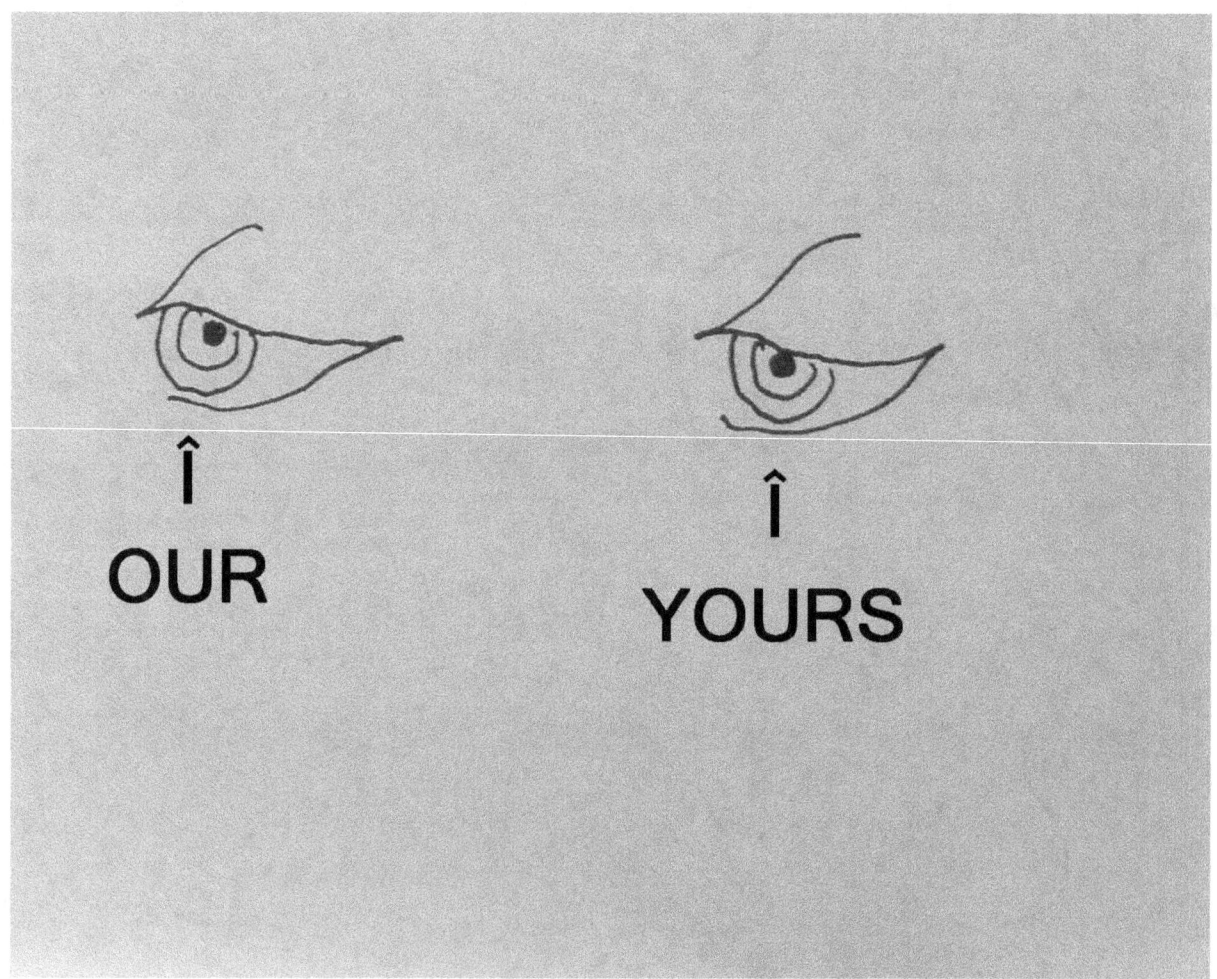

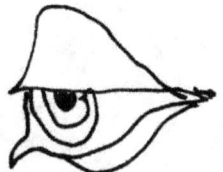

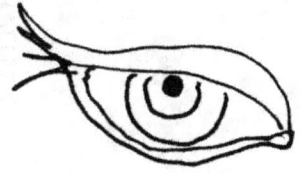

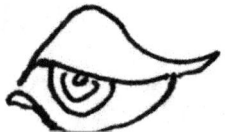

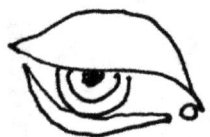

The following pages show how to draw the lips. Draw your lips image on the right, as it shown here:

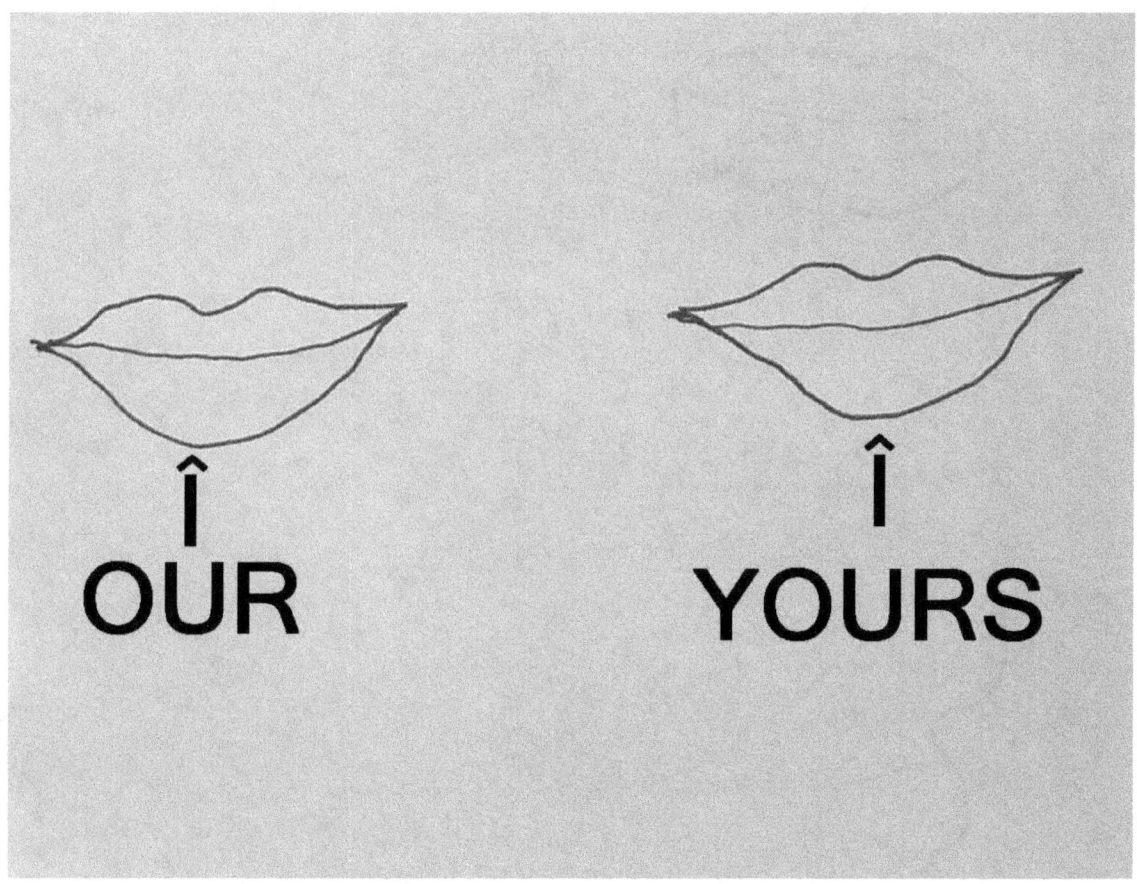

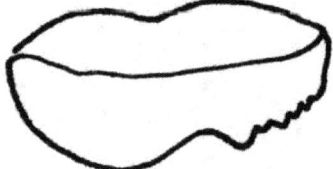

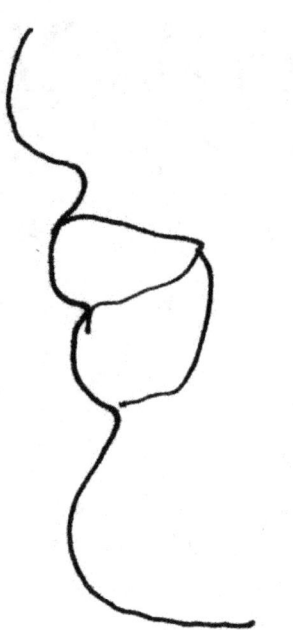

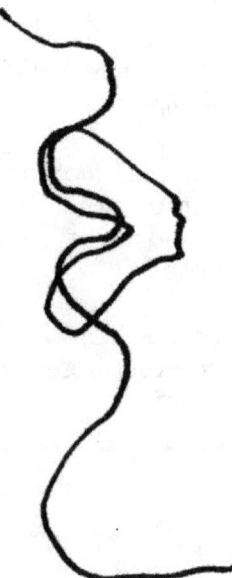

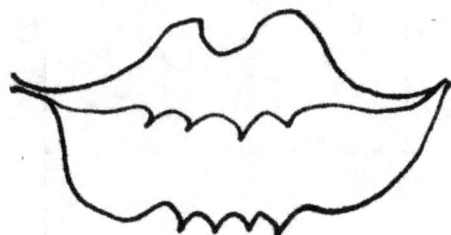

Your repetitive patterns' Gallery

The following pages offer you to create repetitive patterns Gallery. Fill each section with different repetitive pattern as it helps you develop your artistic skills.

Our world is fast and challenging, fun and demanding, exciting and frightening. It produces worry, anxiety, and stress; and we can tolerate only so much of it. Drawing repetitive patterns is rewarding process. It helps you stay calm, bringing your nervous system back into balance, activating your body's relaxation response.

Create patterns using line, circles, squares, ovals, triangles, rectangular; combine them in different variations. Create zigzags, use your imagination. You can use these patterns later in your future ink drawings. Open your mind, impossible is nothing.

1	2	3
4	5	6
7	8	9

10	11	12
13	14	15
16	17	18
19	20	21

22	23	24
25	26	27
28	29	30
31	32	33

34	35	36
37	38	39
40	41	42
43	44	45

46	47	48
49	50	51
52	53	54
55	56	57

58	59	60
61	62	63
64	65	66
67	68	69

70

71

72

73

74

75

76

77

78

79

80

81

82	83	78
79	80	81
82	83	84
85	86	87

88	89	90
91	92	93
94	95	96
97	98	99

Learn to improvise with Nadia Russ

The next pages invite you to learn how to improvise with ink pen. The drawings are like music. They can be happy and sad, mysterious and straight forward. . . When you draw, your draw your mood, your feelings, yourself or people and things you saw and that left trace in your sub-consciousness.

These pages offer Nadia Russ' drawings for you not to copy them (they are copyrighted) but to examine them and learn about different variations you can do with line and repetitive patterns. Remember that eraser is never used because if a 'mistake' made, the following repetitive patterns balance the whole composition.

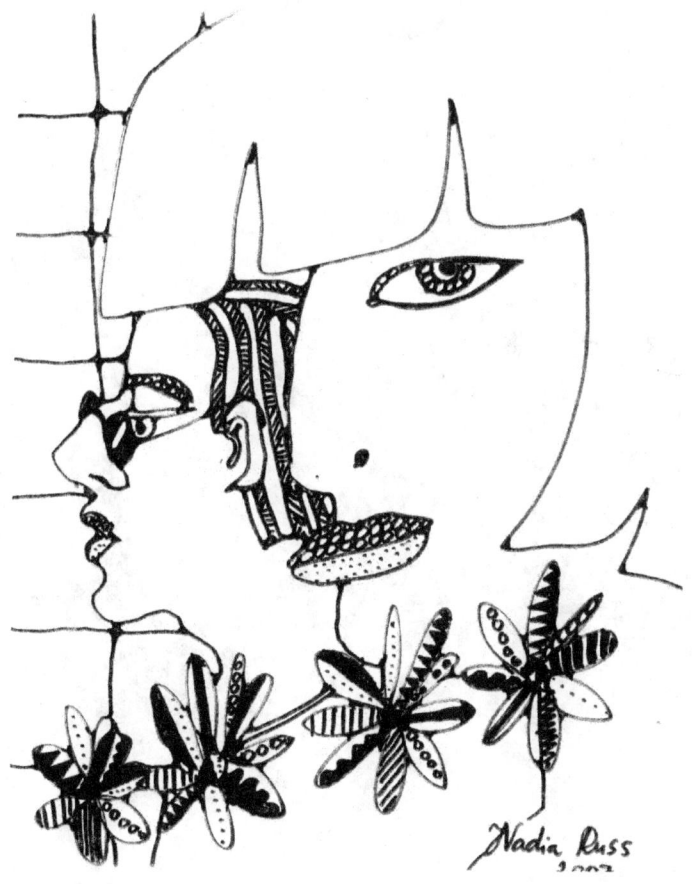

Nadia Russ, *Faces 9*, ink on paper, 8.5"x11", 2007

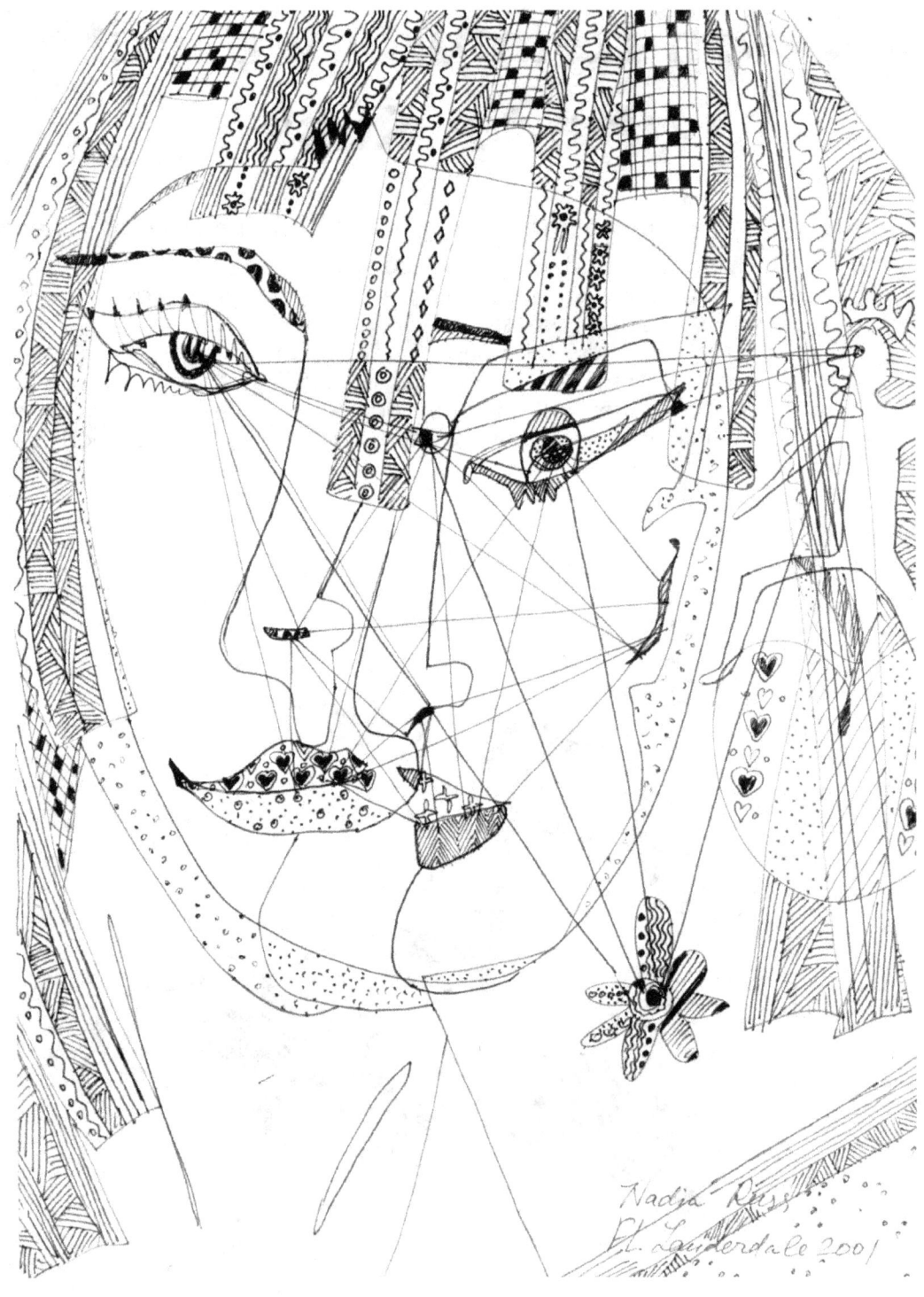

Nadia Russ, *Apple*, ink on paper, 8.5"x10", 2001

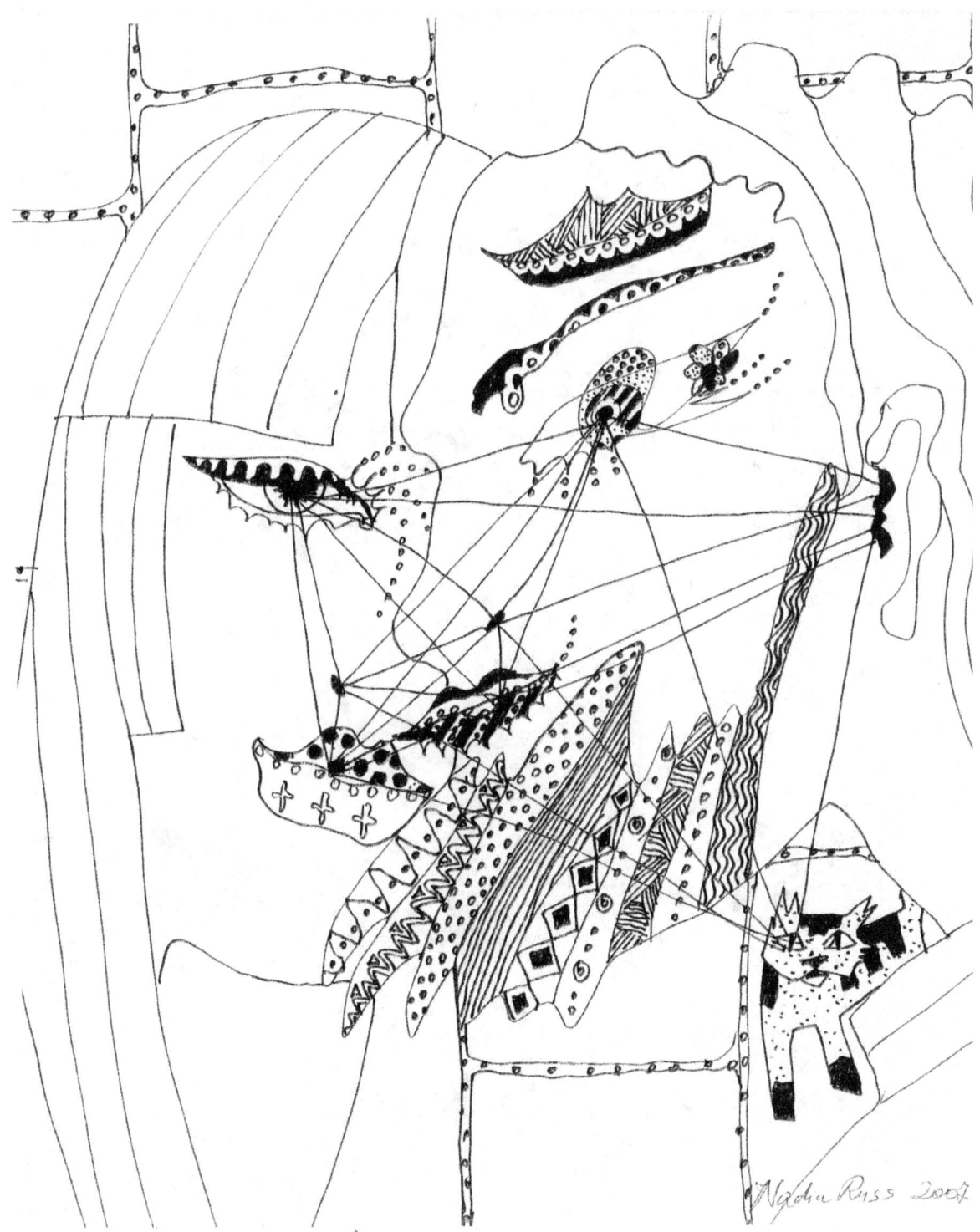

Nadia Russ, *Faces 13*, ink on paper, 7.5"x10", 2007

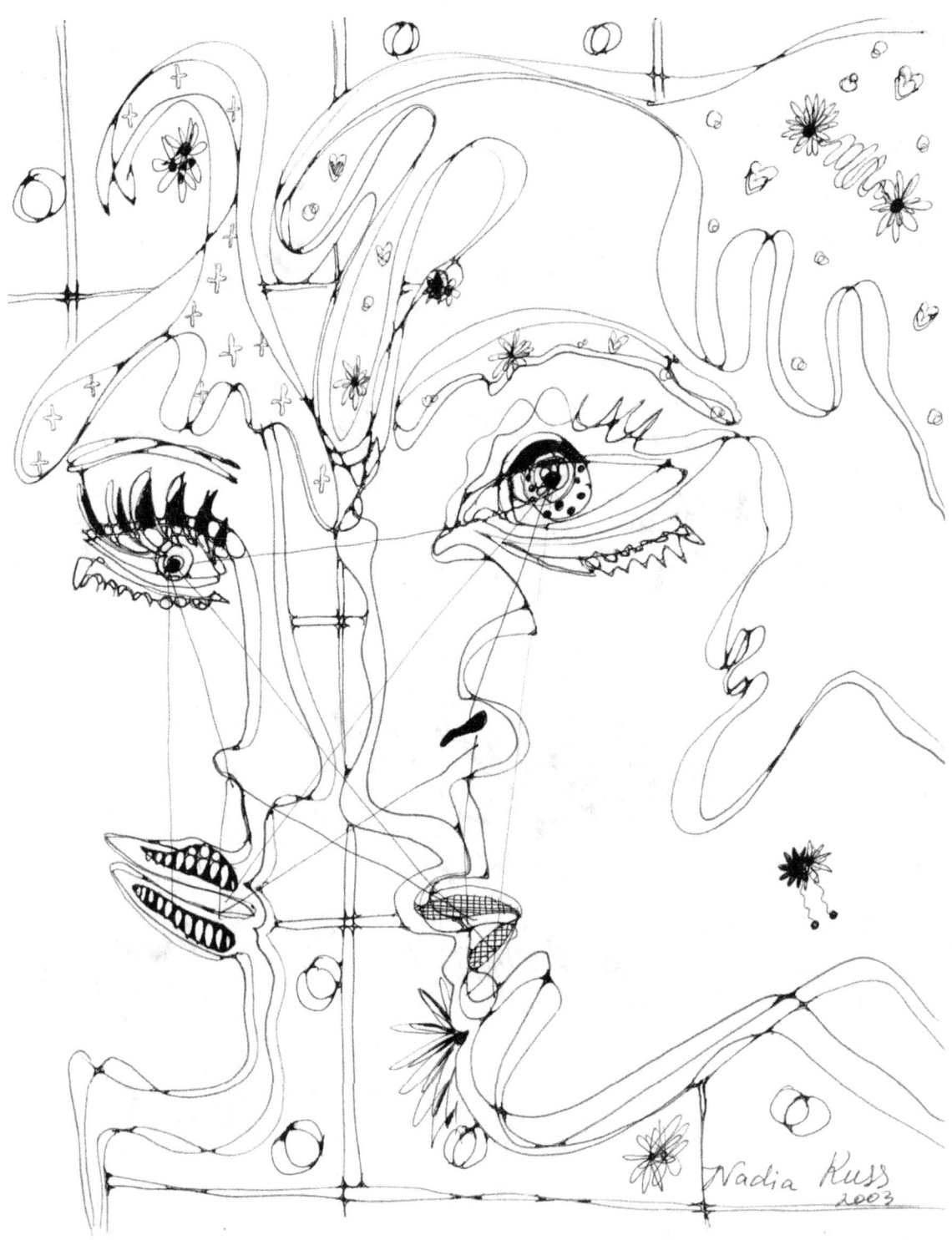

Nadia Russ, *Faces 4*, ink on paper, 8"x11", 2003

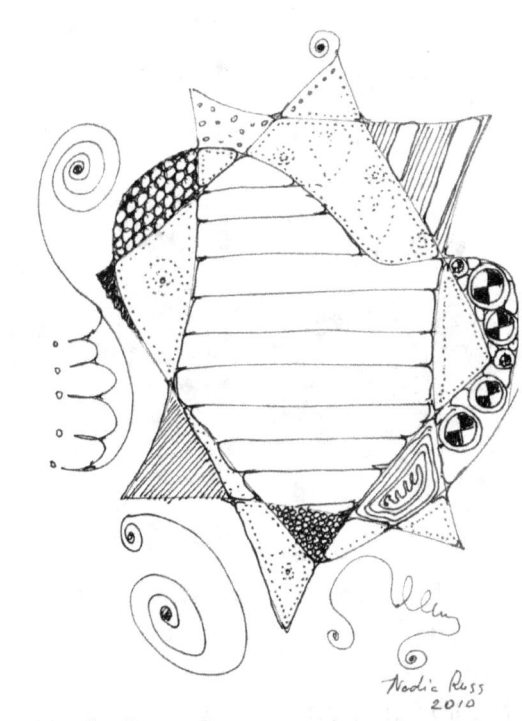

Nadia Russ, *Common*, ink on paper,
5"x10", 2010

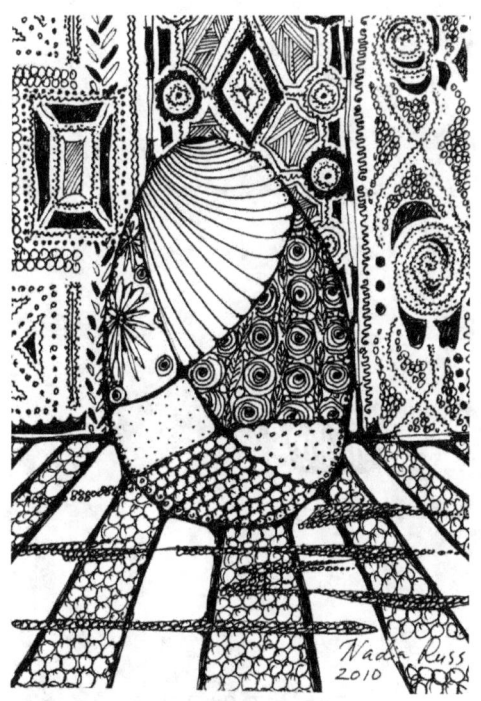

Nadia Russ, *Meditation*, ink on paper,
5"x10", 2010

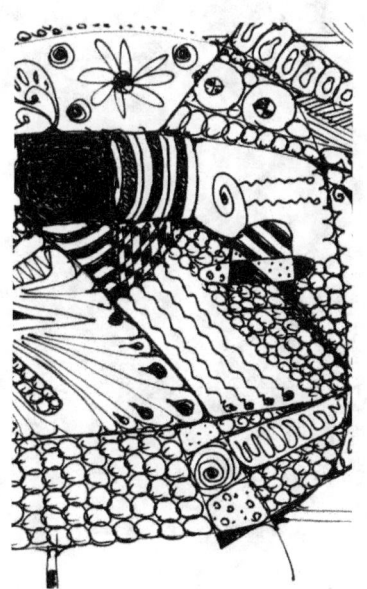

Nadia Russ, *Meditation 1*, ink on paper,
3"x5", 2010

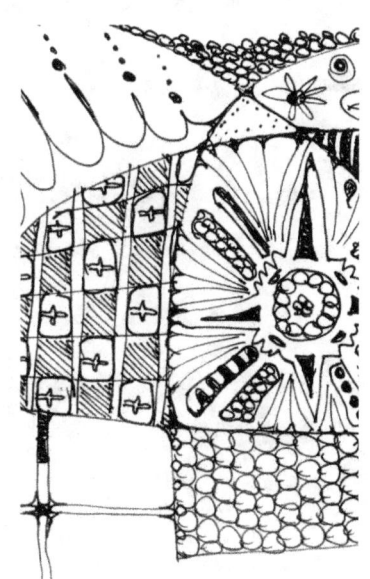

Nadia Russ, *Meditation 2*, ink on paper,
3"x5", 2010

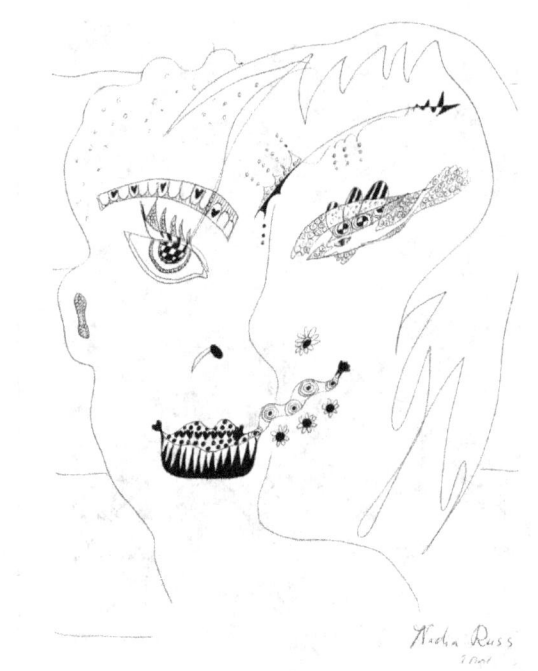

Nadia Russ, *Faces 7*, 8"x11", ink/paper,
winter 2006

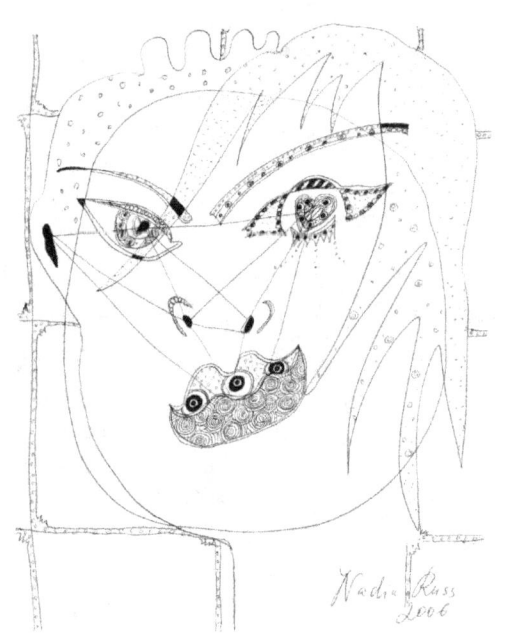

Nadia Russ, *Faces 5*, 8"x11", ink/paper,
winter 2006

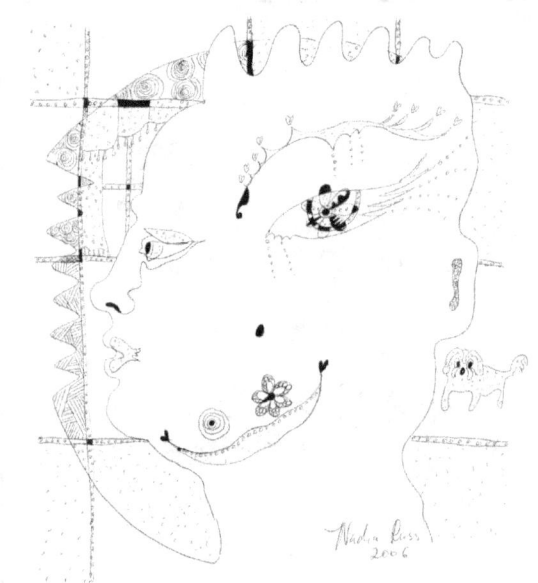

Nadia Russ, *Faces 2*, 8"x11", ink/paper,
winter 2006

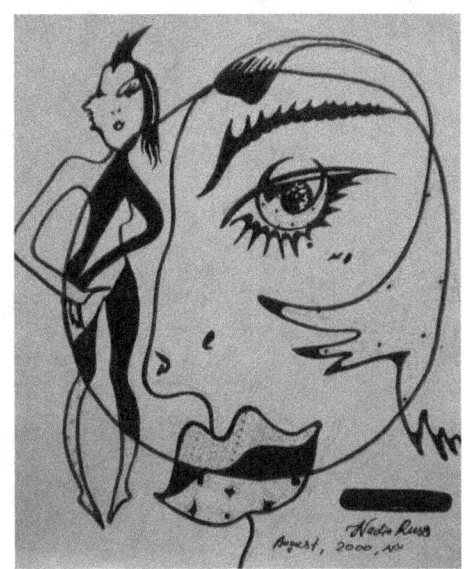

Nadia Russ, *Girl*, 24"x26", ink on paper,
2000

Your exercising pages

These pages are for you to draw your NeoPopRealist images here and now, from its beginning to the end, and show what you learned from this book. Follow all instructions, directions and tips, and, no doubts, you will get the wonderful result. Chose type of the drawing that fits you best - simple or advanced - and enjoy the process!

About NeoPopRealism creator Nadia Russ

Nadia Russ (aka Nadejda Maloletneva) was born into a former professional military officer's family. As a child, she began studying art from famous masters of the past through art books and reproductions, which her mother Vera was collecting in their home. Nadia daily heard about and saw the reproductions of works of Leonardo da Vinci, Michelangelo, Rafael, contemporary Russian artists such as Petrov-Vodkin.

She began painting and drawing seriously in 1989. A few months later, her first ink drawings were exhibited in a group exhibition in famous Moscow's Manege and later, in other Moscow's art galleries. In 1992, she successfully showed her work in New York City.

In 1996-2000, Nadia resided in the Bahamas, where her work gained some special brightness. There, she got her pseudonym to her original 'Nadejda Maloletneva', which was easier to pronounce - 'Nadia Russ'. In 2000-2001, in Xanadu hotel, she operated her Art Gallery Club 13, where she exhibited her acrylic artworks on canvas.

In 2000, she moved to the United States, where she lives up until present. January 4, 2003, Nadia Russ created a word NeoPopRealism and manifested internationally new style of visual arts which combines the brightness and simplicity of Pop Art with deep and psychological realism and has graphic nature. Her artworks are in private and permanent public collections including MOYA - Museum of Young Art in Vienna (Austria), Simferopol and Sumy Art Museums in Ukraine, Kinsey Institute of Indiana University (USA), Ukrainian Museum in New York City (USA), WEAM - World Erotic Art Museum in Miami (USA), Schacknow Museum of Fine Arts (USA), Historical Museum of Fort Lauderdale (USA), Lebedyn and Konotop Art Museums (Ukraine), D. Burliuk Foundation (Ukraine), and other.

In 2008-2010, Nadia Russ founded and juried Int'l NeoPopRealism Starz Art competitions. She authored a few art-related books such as "NeoPopRealism Starz: 21st Century ART" two volumes, "New Millennium ART", "Fort Lauderdale 100: A Must-Have Collector's Edition." She is the founder (2007) of the *NeoPopRealism Journal & Wonderpedia*, publications online, dedicated to arts, culture, books, news, celebrities and more. Nadia Russ lives in New York City and Florida. Visit her website at www.nadiaruss.com.

Conclusion

" W hat is Art?"

Now, when you have learned how to draw the NeoPopRealism ink images, you might have your answer to this open question. We are happy to hear from you, e-mail us to neopoprealism1@yahoo.com. Also, if you have a blog, post there images of your NeoPopRealism ink drawings and a story how you learned to draw them. Have a wonderful journey to the world of NeoPopRealism!

NeoPopRealism ten canons for better and happy living:

1. Be beautiful.
2. Be creative and productive; never stop studying and learning.
3. Be peace-loving, positive-minded.
4. Do not accept communist philosophy.
5. Be free-minded, do the best you can to move the world to peace and harmony.
6. Be family oriented, self-disciplined.
7. Be free spirited. Follow your dreams, if they are not destructive, but constructive.
8. Believe in god. God is one.
9. Be supportive to those who need you, be generous.
10. Create your life as a great adventurous story.

Created by Nadia Russ in 2004.